Journey OF A LIFETIME
—— VOLUME I

MARTIN KARI

Copyright © 2025 Martin Kari.

All rights reserved. No part of this book may be reproduced, stored, or transmitted by any means—whether auditory, graphic, mechanical, or electronic—without written permission of both publisher and author, except in the case of brief excerpts used in critical articles and reviews. Unauthorized reproduction of any part of this work is illegal and is punishable by law.

ISBN: 978-1-63950-361-2 (sc)
ISBN: 978-1-63950-362-9 (hc)
ISBN: 978-1-63950-367-4 (e)

Because of the dynamic nature of the Internet, any web addresses or links contained in this book may have changed since publication and may no longer be valid. The views expressed in this work are solely those of the author and do not necessarily reflect the views of the publisher, and the publisher hereby disclaims any responsibility for them.

Gateway Towards Success

8063 MADISON AVE #1252
Indianapolis, IN 46227
+13176596889
www.writersapex.com

CONTENTS

About the Author v
Dedication vii
Note ix
Prologue—Journey of a Lifetime xi

Journey Begins 1
    World War II – Transylvania 1
    Escape 7
    Refuge in Germany 10

Life Continues 12
    First settlement Weilderstadt 12
    Settlement Rotenbach 20
    Settlement Weissenstein 34
    Settlement Ettlingen 37

Life Improves – School Years 42
    Boy scouts and music 42
    Hospital 45
    Sports 48

First Journeys 52
    Germany – Denmark 52
    'Tour de France' 57
    Work Experience 62

Apprentice years 69
    The Alps 73
    Berlin 75
    Dance School 81
    Black Forest 86
    Black Forest tour 89
    Oberkochen 93
    Southern France 97

New Horizons – Work Life, Studies 111
- Matriculation 111
- Scandinavia 113
- Paris is always worth it 123
- Heidelberg 127
- Finland visit 129
- Terror in Germany 135
- Morocco 137
- London 161
- Arja – first Germany visit 165
- Amsterdam 169
- Around the Mediterranean 173
- Austria – Yugoslavia – Bulgaria 174
- Turkey 174
- Syria 179
- Lebanon 182
- Egypt 186
- Libya 219
- Tunisia 228
- Algeria 232
- Morocco 234
- Spain 235
- France 236
- Germany 236
- Stockholm, Sweden 237
- Engagement 238

Epilogue 245

ABOUT THE AUTHOR

The author Martin Kari was born during World War Two in 1941 in Transylvania. He spent his first 26 years 'travelling': First as a refugee in Germany, then going through different education levels, working life, country travels and many hobbies.

Other stages of his life include marrying Arja and raising six children. They continued the journey together travelling and living throughout the world before finally settling in Australia in 1981. This book concludes with his engagement to Arja. The family's life story continues in Martin's next book: *Journey of a Lifetime, Volume Two*.

DEDICATION

To my dearest wife, **Arja Kari**—

You are the heart of every journey I have taken, the quiet strength behind every step, and the joy that has made each moment worth living.

When the road was long, your love carried me.
When doubts crept in, your faith steadied me.
When the world felt uncertain, your presence was my home.

This book is not just my story—it is ours. The laughter, the tears, the miles we have traveled together are woven into every page. Without you, the journey would have been empty. With you, it has been a lifetime of wonder, love, and belonging.

Arja, my love, my partner, my forever—everything I am, and everything I write, is because of you.

With endless gratitude and devotion,

Martin

NOTE

Some of the personal names included in this book have been changed, or only first names have been included, to protect the privacy of those concerned.

PROLOGUE— JOURNEY OF A LIFETIME

A journey in our lives is like a dream come true. It is also a biography and an account of one's life which is full of surprises.

We never know what lies ahead. Nothing is more interesting than an individual's life. And life is our best teacher. Writing and reading about a person's life enables us to enter into an open dialogue with others.

Every 'journey of a lifetime' is also a document of time. The values of a lifetime journey are equal—no journey can claim to be the better one.

Here is the first part of my life. Belonging to a stolen generation and starting under difficult conditions could not stop my journey being a colourful one. I have experienced the Second World War in Transylvania; youth as a refugee in Germany; the slow recovery after the war; 'normalisation' with education, boyish pranks, boy scouts, sports, music, work, journeys in between, controversies, romances, a love story, successes and starting to go out into the world.

I have documented my many travel experiences and share these in following pages with my readers. Here, meeting people takes centre stage with all of its positive and negative experiences.

Questions arise on the way through life. My philosophy of a 'journey of a lifetime' remains a reliable partner never falling short of answers to my endless questions.

I invite you to read this chapter of my life story—never fail to keep a good smile ready.

The author

Martin Kari, 2007

Journey Begins

World War II – Transylvania

My father Michael Lutsch turned up unexpectedly late in the summer of 1944 in Sibiu, the capital of Transylvania.

It was World War Two. Nobody would have thought that during this war time somebody could escape from a concentration camp alive. But my father did.

The whole population of Transylvania got caught up in the war machine in those years – right from the beginning of the war. It is a historic dilemma that Transylvania never managed, in its 850 years of history, to establish an independent territory in its own right. Romania, the governing authority during that time, decided unopposed to supply prisoners of war to the invader from the north, Russia, to avoid direct war conflict. Transylvania was next in line, so everybody who was caught at home, in the street or at work, female or male, regardless of age, had to follow the long miserable journey to Siberia. Not many returned from there and, if they did, they were marked for the rest of their lives.

In such an environment it came as no surprise that the news of my father's sudden return arrived before him in town.

What would be the most natural thing for a father to do in those circumstances? To find out what was left of his family, of course. Small children could not be easily deported. His two boys, aged five and three, must have been somewhere. With this in mind, my father headed straight to the city of Sibiu after he could not find any trace of his two boys in his home town of Seica Mica.

Hailing from an established family who had farmed the area for many generations, my father quickly found information about his boys' whereabouts. The trail in his search for Martin led to Sibiu and the home of very 'noble citizens' of this town. My father presented himself at the home, saying: "I am the father of the boy Martin, who I understand is in your care. I would like to know how he is."

Instead of an answer, the door was slammed in his face. From behind the door he heard: "You idiot farmer go to the hell." And this from 'honorable, highly-educated' people. My father had no answer to this. He just turned away and headed back to his farm.

More pressing things were awaiting him. During his absence, gypsies had settled on his property. Despite this, he could find a roof over his head and his determination to reclaim his farm remained unchanged. He eventually gained the upper hand and reclaimed his property, but only after a massive fight. Father Michael had his property back and he was a proud farmer again, even though the property was left in a deplorable condition.

His pride was bitter sweet as he was alone and did not have his sons. He had managed to escape from the brutal concentration camp and regain his farm – the only one in the small town of Seica Mica. But now he had to get his family back. Where were his two boys Michael and Martin? Tragic memories came flooding back of the time, when he lost his wife, Sara, during childbirth with their second son, Martin, on June 22, 1941.

Seica Mica, (Kleinschelken) church-castle, Transylvania

That summer had promised a good harvest. Corn stood high and rich on the fields ready for harvesting. In times without war, plenty of hands became available to bring in the harvest. The farming community of Transylvania was highly organised and self-sufficient. Part of a harvest was always stored away in a unique fortress that is found only in Transylvania – an architectural combination of a church within a citadel.

For centuries, the population of these small communities in Transylvania survived many outside aggressions by sheltering in those 'church-castles'.

Such a defence tradition, however, proved to become an isolating factor for this community over the generations.

I should come back briefly to the high organisation of the farming community in Transylvania. During harvest time, child care centres were formed and some women voluntarily looked after the children, while every other available adult worked in the field to bring in the harvest.

My birthday, June 22, 1941, was not a normal peacetime day. The Russians had crossed the Romanian border that day. Transylvania's alliance with the Nazi regime was not welcomed by Russia. War bells were ringing throughout the country, particularly in the north where Transylvania shares the border with the Goliath, Russia. Romania was not in a position to stand up to such provocation. This situation created widespread government corruption reaching all the way to the King at the top. The government then made a mistake by asking the Nazis for help. The whole country found itself in total disarray.

In the midst of this confusion, my mother found herself giving birth to her second child – me. On this day of my birth, all the men were called to arms and so my mother, Sara, was on her own when her confinement started. Nobody really knows what happened. Somehow I survived, but my mother succumbed to the consequences of this birth and died soon after.

There is no record of how my life started. This motherless baby boy must have been swapped from one relative to another – to whoever could find time to look after me.

Despite war raging in the country, people still had to sustain their lives. The harvest had to be prepared and brought in. The summer of 1944 proved very difficult to sow and harvest. The war claimed lots of men and women so only a very reduced work-force was available. People came from other districts to help out in childcare centres during the harvest.

The district capital of Mediasch struggled to cope with an influx of children from its districts. I was not the only child who had nobody to look after him. A lady came to help out from as far away as Busteni, a small town in the Carpathian mountains with a natural southern border to Romania.

One of the many tasks with these children became toilet training. Generally such sessions lasted until a successful result became evident, this was waiting time. The lady from Busteni filled in such time with stories.

I was fascinated by these stories and so was not in a hurry to do my loo business.

This lady from the mountains attracted my attention, because she wore shiny rings in the middle of both hands.

I could not resist holding these hands while sitting on my loo pot and listening to this beautiful lady's stories. Such a waiting session could not last long enough for me. When the lady made an attempt to move somewhere else, I started holding her firmly by the hand. There must have been some kind of affection in the air.

After just a few days the lady took me away from the childcare centre. I was too young to understand what was going on. The journey to the mountains did not start before I was dressed with new clothes – a new experience in my young life. The journey on the train to Sibiu was exciting. I made sure I didn't miss anything that flew past the windows. Everything was new: People, houses, the whole carriage of the train. It didn't take long to fall asleep. This journey continued from Sibiu in a car, which the lady's husband was driving into the mountains to Busteni.

A short and wonderful time started here for me. A villa with my own room, a marvellous garden, everything so nice and perfect. A few days later the war reached Mediasch and the childcare centre was bombed. No child survived. What a lucky fate I had! As I enjoyed my role in such a new life, the circle of time caught up with the event when my father Michael paid his visit to a family member of these new foster parents. This was when he was thrown out. The ball of events kept rolling. In times of war many things of daily life are barely functional and people are forced into survival mode.

This father's visit in Sibiu and his request for his son quickly reached my new foster parents in Busteni.

Out of fear that something could change this 'happy family life', panic took over. According to stories that were told later, my stepfather Peter rushed home one day and it was decided to leave everything behind and immediately join a train, which was evacuating German troops from Romania. The ground must have become hot, and not only because of the war, to make such hasty decision.

As soon as communication stops, panic begins. Some 34 years later, I met my father for the first time thanks to the work of the Red Cross. He had nothing else to say but: "Why was I left for so long in the dark about the fate of my second son, Martin? I raised my first son, Michael, and another four children in a new marriage with the sister of my first wife, Sara. I have enough children. I wanted only to know how my son Martin was. Why is the world like this?"

Chances of a better understanding were missed. The villain in us makes us think the other is a bigger villain. Social barriers contribute so often to a wrong understanding. I refer to the confrontation with 'higher society' when my father went to look for me in Sibiu.

If we manage to break down such social barriers we can only learn from developing an open dialogue with other people. Misunderstandings are the most common ingredients of conflict in our world. It has always been like this and I doubt whether it will change.

The course of events was given a direction. How much was wanted or unwanted, it was like a gamble in uncertain times of war.

Martin, Busteni, Transylvania, 1944

Escape

The train took me, my stepmother Heidi and stepfather Peter on board at the station in Busteni. There was no time to get familiar with this environment. After a very short stop, the steam train continued its journey to the west. This was a very different train from that first trip to Busteni. In the middle of each carriage were two big sliding doors, no windows; very different from a train with bench compartments and windows to look out. A number of other people were on that train with us. Each carriage had a small platform under a domed roof connecting to the next carriage.

Before this train left Busteni, a small mattress had to be organised in a hurry, and due to this we nearly missed the train's departure. The floor of the train carriages was of plain timber. This journey had its incidents, but I was thankfully too young to remember.

The Allies under the command of the American military allowed the train to leave Romania, but only to travel to the west with its load of mainly German military personnel.

Goods-train leaving Busteni, 1944

Russia was pressing ahead with its war machine in this part of the world and did not tolerate a German military presence here.

The different nature of this train also became evident with armed American forces occupying each platform between the carriages. Food was not available, however it was obvious that the Americans on the platforms were receiving regular tin food.

The train only travelled at night to avoid becoming a target for fighter planes. Once the train stopped, nobody was allowed to leave the carriages. The military guards strictly enforced this. As I cannot remember these days, I don't know what happened on this journey. People must have become desperate, out of hunger. It was cold and the carriages offered very little protection. There was a door leading out of the carriage to the platform between two carriages. This door had the only window and you could see the guard on the platform. The smell of tin food wafted agonizingly into the carriages. Somebody was said to have opened the door and grabbed half an empty tin of food that was abandoned by a guard, before it eventually rolled off the platform on to the track. The guard was not asleep, he got up on his feet, pulled his gun and shot the 'could-be-thief'. The train had to stop, the 'thief' was thrown out and the journey carried on. No more sudden movements became the new rule. But despite this shooting, people still left the train when it stopped. It became a daily event. People were driven to such actions either because of hunger, sickness or mental outburst. What a gamble this train journey became! On one occasion, just before the border of Austria, aircraft targeted our train in the middle of the night. The train stopped. This time people were told to flee into the nearby cornfields for their own safety. The train driver was the only person killed and that was when a bomb hit the steam engine. Everybody else had survived in the cornfields, but the train had neither an engine nor a driver.

Somehow it was organised for another steam engine to come to the rescue and push our train over the border into Austria. This phantom rail journey had taken two weeks and the passengers were in a miserable condition.

Austria was another country and our hopes were raised, but the officials decided to hose this miserable group of passengers with a water gun from tanks that were used to fill the steam engine's tank. Some weak people collapsed on the spot from the force of the water. Such a cleaning idea was radical and not the norm. How I survived this train journey, I don't know. Because I was so young, I do not remember such a difficult time.

The other passengers must have wondered, why a new mother and her husband were leaving Transylvania without their wider families. As it turned out, my step-parents' fears that I would be found by my father were unfounded. He never did contact anybody from this family after his visit to Sibiu.

To get clearance into the refugee camp, my step-parents had to fill out some paperwork and have a basic medical check up.

Refuge in Germany

As my stepfather Peter could provide an address of his sister's family in Germany, we did not have to stay for very long in the camp. Soon we were on a train journey to Germany. Everything became new and exciting to me.

This train journey reminded us that the war was raging in Germany as well. German military security personnel randomly checked people everywhere, but never said what they were looking for.

Such actions made the passengers very insecure. Nobody was talking. Everybody knew that these security officers were looking for 'enemies of the Reich'. Newcomers like us had to be very careful in everything we did and said.

As Transylvania was officially on the side of Germany, we were not subjected to unnecessary scrutiny. A German-sounding name and coming from a highly traditional German background was, for the time being, good enough for the authorities.

Exiled Germans are known to cling to their German tradition, very often with more fervour than their fellow citizens in Germany.

The current generation in Transylvania was still using the Saxon dialect, as this was spoken in the area of today's Luxemburg some 800 years ago. Our Saxon dialect did not help our situation, because it immediately identified us as refugees – and in war times refugees have a very difficult time.

Life Continues

First settlement Weilderstadt

Our train journey ended in the small town of Weilderstadt, near the city of Stuttgart. Peter's sister, Kathy, lived with her family on a hillside overlooking Weilderstadt. They were tenants of an old man, Mr Letsche, and occupied a room under the gable. We could not stay there for very long. Nobody could afford to be a burden on somebody else.

Weilderstadt – Germany, Martin and 3 cousins, 1945

Food was scarce, everything was rationed with food tickets, which were very difficult to get and had limited use.

I did enjoy the company of the three children of Kathy and Hans, whose names were Elisabeth, Doris and Fred. The two girls were older than me, Fred was still a baby. My memory set in from that time, which means that everything I am writing from now on is based on my own memories.

Our stay in Weilderstadt was going to be short because we had to look for our own way of life. While stepfather Peter looked for work, our daily lives passed happily. Kathy preoccupied us four children with a program of her own so that nobody thought any more about the difficult war situation around us.

Toys did not exist. A kite was created from only a few insignificant materials. After playtime, our living area was cleaned up and then our reading lessons took off on a blackboard. We then went out to the road, which led into the fields outside the town. Kathy and stepmother Heidi were always with us. An hour or two passed virtually unnoticed, while everybody tried their kite-flying skills.

Even the rain did not stop us going out. A plastic raincoat provided the required protection, but the kite had to be left behind. Instead we could learn about what grew along the roadside: field flowers and leaves of clover. Who was going to find the four-leafed clover that would bring us luck? One rainy day we had to stop and return home.

On a previous day we collected blueberries from a nearby forest. Food supplements were a necessity on our table. Every time after a daily excursion, something came on our table—not much—but hunger was always our best cook.

One hour of sleep in the early afternoon became the daily rule. The remaining hours of the day were dedicated to small tasks indoors and outdoors.

The landlord Mr Letsche demanded peace and quiet during the day and this was a strict requirement.

A glasshouse was attached to the house, where our landlord spent most of his time cultivating a variety of vegetables.

No other person was ever seen in his glasshouse, which was his domain. Our room under the gable connected with a platform to this glasshouse and Mr Letsche allowed us, from our room, to watch him grow his vegetables. Some of his vegetables came on our table in exchange for other goods.

Then father Peter's sudden recruitment into the German army changed our life. Mother Heidi had to find something to do to bring food onto our table.

There was no work, especially for refugees during the war. She found ways to get food. The only people who had food during those times were the farmers in town.

Money became worthless with the constant rise in inflation. People exchanged gold, watches and the like for very little food. We could not trade food on such a basis. Mother Heidi could trade with her skills. She offered a farmer's family in town to knit baby clothes for their grandchild, if they supplied the materials. Money was even of no use for the farmers to buy goods, so her work was very welcome. The grandchild could not have a better deal, it being so close to winter. Mother Heidi's 'foot was in the door'. Then a room under the roof in the farmhouse became available and help with farm work was also accepted. No further questions were asked.

Life definitely looked brighter for the two of us. The farm had a few milk cows, chickens, some geese, and, in the basement of the opposite building a number of pigs were kept. A shed between the two buildings was ready to be filled with hay for the coming winter.

Daily life started now for us on this farm. There was no money, but there were other natural options like a roof over our heads, food on the table and special skills attracting the exchange of other goods.

A seemingly useless corner of a field outside town caught mum's eye. She had plans to cultivate vegetables for our own use and the farmers did not object. The use of this patch of land seemed very much restricted, because a lot of rubbish had been dumped there. Considering that mother Heidi's profession was a teacher in mathematics, she managed this new life situation extremely competently.

At the end of 1944 the war came closer to everybody's door-steps. Routines of daily life became more and more interrupted through air-raid warnings. When sirens filled the air, everything stopped, people rushed to the closest civil bunker.

An incredible number of bombers delivered a constant deep sound out of the sky. Other towns like Pforzheim, Stuttgart and Freudenstadt were targeted. I remember on one occasion, the civil air-raid bunker under the fire brigade house, which was close to us, was filled with people when we arrived in the middle of the night. The noise out of the sky reached us while we were waiting on the stairs which led down to the bunker. We could observe the moment when a 'Christmas tree' dropped from a bomber. These were bright bombs used to illuminate the area for the bomber pilot's observation. Our town remained insignificant as a military target. Before people could leave the relative safety of a civil bunker, the target became apparent on the horizon. A whole city must have gone up in fire – the city of Pforzheim was on its way to being wiped off the map. The air raids were more frequent that night, the Allies intensified the assault.

Next day, our town was filled with deadly silence. Everybody knew what had happened the night before.

As long as the sirens were silent, daily business could be pursued.

My first task started early in the morning. Mum handed me the milk can and the official food-stamp card. On the corner, just across the road, a shop distributed milk. Mum put me in the queue and asked me to keep my position so that she could do something else more useful during this waiting game. A fat, bald man sat in an elevated room behind a desk, the top of his white apron clearly visible. The milk can, full of milk for distribution, sat next to him but was not visible to the waiting queue. Very rarely I came face to face with this big man, usually mum arrived just in time to take over this waiting game. The milk in the can was not properly stirred. The top level of the can was the thinner blue-white milk. It was the lower level of the can which contained the thicker part of the milk. The man would only lower his ladle deep into the milk can if you did him a favour. When I collected the milk, somebody around me had to help me make my presence visible. As a young child, I could not appear in front of this big, fat man. As a result, I only received the blue milk from the top. I was afraid of this man, but I did not know why.

For various reasons, the milk ran short on certain days, so many people in the queue wasted their time. "No milk anymore", came the call from the big, bald man behind the desk. Most people were aware of what really went on. Preferred customers were given a milk supply behind closed doors. But during war and in uncertain times, nobody really wanted to stand up for justice, when injustice dominated. So we all accepted the milk supply situation.

But this big man's power did not last forever. Soon after the end of the war, when normality started to take a foothold, the people of Weilderstadt stood up against this abuse of power. The big milk man ended up in jail. As an old family saying goes: "A jug goes to the well for as long until it breaks."

The military presence interrupted town life occasionally.

Foreign soldiers combed houses for hidden Nazis sometimes in the middle of the night.

On such an occasion I saw for the first time a black man—an American soldier. Luck remained on our side, we were left unharmed. Mum reminded the soldier of his family far away.

In the weeks before winter, mother Heidi spent every available hour working up the dumping field into a small garden of Eden.

A variety of vegetables found their way on the table with the farmer's family. We were occasionally invited for dinner with the farmer. A big clay pot sat in the middle of the table. The farmer's wife scooped food into each plate on the table. We were served first, and it did not escape my attention that the top of the pot ended up on the plate as a very watery soup with some fat potato eyes swimming around. The next servings were from the bottom of the pot – chunky meat and potato pieces. I could not hide my surprise and pointed to this difference. Hunger was in these days a driving force. The farmer's wife must have become embarrassed about such openness from a child. She answered quickly: "Have some more so that you can become a strong man." Nobody was happier than me. My stomach at last got something to work on.

We had to look after ourselves most of the days. One day mum brought two white eggs on to the table. While preparing a meal, she said: "If the mother hen sits long enough on the eggs, baby chickens will hatch". Her words preoccupied my mind, which created fantasy pictures. When fried eggs were served on the table, I strongly refused to eat. The poor little chicken that could have hatched was on my mind. Mum became very sad about this situation. Chicken babies were prevented from hatching and at the same time this food could not serve its purpose – to feed me. There was not much of a choice in food during that time. Mum only told me later that she tricked me into eating the eggs by mashing them together with potatoes. She did not say one word and was finally happy to see how little Martin did eat with a good appetite the next day.

Late summer 1945 had been sunny and it rained very little. Hay could still be brought in during October. On such a harvesting day mum had to put the horse to the wagon, go out to the fields and collect the dry hay before the rain set in. I only could watch how the bales piled up on the wagon. The horse was feeding on oats out of a bay attached to his halter. A storm was brewing on the horizon and we had to hurry home before the rain started. With the bales of hay securely stacked on the wagon, mum was just about to grab the reins and help me climb up from the horse's thill to settle high into the hay. All of a sudden our horse took off, it must have been startled by thunder. Mum just managed to hang on to the thill. With her left hand she secured me in the hay, with her right she pulled as hard as she could on the reins of the horse, shouting "whoa, whoa, whoa" to stop the horse in its gallop. The dirt road was to the left – the right side of the road centre dug out unevenly by wagon wheels. Our horse was in full gallop heading towards the town. Mum was very worried – would our horse slow down before the tower into town? Then a miracle happened: Mum was still pulling hard on the reins, holding her balance on the thill, shouting repeatedly as loud as possible "whoa, whoa, whoa". Finally our horse slowed down and we continued our ride with the horse at a gentle trot. Mum was very relieved. She was only now prepared to admit how lucky we were that the wagon did not turn over on that rutted dirt road. As a child I thought this wild ride was fun. I could not comprehend the danger we were in and mum's astonishing courage.

Time went on. We heard very little from dad, who became caught in the war machine as a prisoner. A bit more than a year had to pass to bring in May 1946, the end of this war and my dad's imprisonment. He returned to us very skinny, but with a strong determination to move on and make a good life. Life on the farm started to change for us. Dad had old contacts from the time before the war and one in particular with an influential industrial boss called Dr Engineer Heller. The trail to this gentleman led to Weissenstein, a suburb of Pforzheim. Dad found this contact in a paper manufacturing place. Mr Heller told dad before the war: "When you ever need a job as a chemistry engineer, come and see me." So it was now that dad went to see him. Mr Heller kept his promise, a remarkable attitude which was not very common in those times.

The factory in Weissenstein was in ruins like everything else from the war. Dr Heller met dad in the plant at Weissenstein. The meeting was transferred to a restaurant, one of the few still functional. Despite everybody being stripped of everything because of the war, Dr Heller managed to secure whatever he found necessary. He invited dad to drive with him in his car to a restaurant in a small town further out in the country. Nobody else could even think of owning a car at that time, but Dr Heller not only had a car but also a chauffeur.

It was a small truck with a stove right behind the cabin. The stove was used to run the truck and was fuelled by dry timber (a timber carburetion motor). Dr Heller always took goods with him that he could exchange for other goods or services. In this instance, Dr Heller first went to the back door of the restaurant to exchange goods and then used the official front entrance. With no questions asked, a complete dinner arrived – a rarity in post-war times when nothing was available.

The outcome of that dinner party was an agreement to start a manufacturing plant near Rotenbach to supply cellulose to make paper. The small cellulose grinding plant was in one of the valleys close to Weissenstein. It was dad's challenge to rebuild this mechanical pulping machine from out of ruins. Thus we had to move to a new home near Rotenbach in the middle of the Enz valley. Dr. Heller made it possible for us to start a new life.

We left the farmer's place in Weilderstadt and Mr Heller sent his personal driver to pick us up. We had so little possessions of our own, we could move immediately. Before we left Weilderstadt, mum suggested we pay a quick visit to the small field she had been cultivating outside town to see what food we could take with us. We were in a bit of a hurry and when people in other fields saw our car and saw Dad rush to collect the vegetables, they shouted: "The lady, who works this field, has done such an effort to grow these vegetables, you can't take them away like this."

Then Mum stepped out of the small truck and explained our situation to these people. We were very grateful for their protection of mum's vegetables. We then continued our drive to our new residence in Rotenbach.

Settlement Rotenbach

After leaving the conditions in Weilderstadt, the lonely buildings further up the river Enz from the village Rotenbach invited us into a different life. In my eyes, the house looked huge – wide stairs led from ground level to an entrance hall. A number of doors indicated entrances to other rooms, which were all empty. That is why all the rooms looked big. In one corner of this floor level lived an old lady, Mrs Huber. She did not hide her joy that her lonely life was going to change.

While mum and dad inspected the empty rooms, Mrs Huber called me into her room, which was stylish furnished. She lived on her own, dressed in black clothes and offered me a sweet, which I could not refuse. This lady was very kind and talked a lot to me. When I left her to see mum and dad, I had to promise to come back and visit again. To make my visits more attractive, she offered a sweet each time.

Mum and dad had a lot to do to get our life started from virtually nothing. Buying something was not an option, there were neither money nor shops. Time during summer helped us to overcome some of these shortfalls. Dad faced a huge task in the factory downstairs. The demolished place had to be somehow fixed quickly to produce the cellulose for Mr Heller's factory in Weissenstein. On the side of the building there was a channel with a barrage. From here a water wheel took water into its scoops to drive a shaft installation, which entered the factory floor.

The big house with its three floor levels, together with a smaller house next door were located on an island formed between the river Enz and the branched-off channel. Further down, just before the small village of Rotenbach, the channel converged with river Enz. Typical Black Forest landscape covered a line of hills on both sides of this valley. At the southern foot of these hills, close to our house, was the railway line which carried only a few trains every day.

A road connected this valley with the outside world to the north and down stream.

The war was officially over. Military units still moved through our valley. One day big numbers of tanks rolled through our road.

Their engines roared through the entire valley with incredible noise. Men with motorised saws arrived as well. For days the saws cut down the forest above the road by day and night. The mighty force of the tanks pulled the trunks on to the road, bundled them together with chains and dragged them away. The constant noise became unbearable and when the forest had disappeared, the road became impassable.

These military personnel spoke French. They came several times to our house asking for all sorts of things. As mum and dad could communicate very well in their language, freedom remained in our place. This brutal deforestation was an action of the Allied Forces on their retreat. When the tanks left, peace came back to our valley and normal duties returned.

One major duty was the garden. To get something out of the grass land around the house required a lot of hard work: removing the grass, digging deep for loose soil, picking up all the rocks and hilling up the soil in even rows. All garbage from the kitchen was composted into the soil plus everything else, what we could get hands on: chicken manure, cow manure, sheep manure, straw – no matter how little, everything went to prepare the soil for a variety of seeds. Our lives depended very much on such efforts. The amount we could grow was the amount we could feed ourselves. The government supplied food-stamp cards but they were in limited supply.

A few years on, 'Gaensbrunnenwiese' (or Geeswell Meadows) as this place between the two divided streams was called, brought a degree of stability into our lives.

For a young boy of my age (I was six years old in 1947), such a place offered an 'El Dorado' for activities. Television would not be a reality for 10 years. Even a radio remained out of reach for most people in those early days after the war. News was relayed from person to person. Newspapers were rare. The war brought the fate of all down to one level, from where life started for each individual again.

There was always much to do and never enough to eat. A comment from dad in later years was: "In the time after the war, people were neither fat nor sick".

Back to Geeswell Meadows; as soon as our vegetable garden began to flourish, we made a rule: Whoever came to see us and put his foot under our table received first a spade to make himself useful in our garden. Nobody could afford to feed somebody else without a proper contribution.

Mum went usually to Neuenburg once a week, a place bigger than Rotenbach and further upstream on the River Enz. The road had no traffic those days. Mum could pull a small wagon to bring home the items that the foodstamp cards allowed us to receive. I had already joined school in Rotenbach. When school finished early, mum would take me on the trip to Neuenburg. While mum pulled the wagon along the road, I sat in the wagon most of the time. The existence of this wagon had a history. Dad came home one day with a letter from the local council which said we were eligible for assistance and could have a wagon. Curious as I was, I wanted to know what such a wagon looked like. From dad's description

I believed the wagon had four wheels. After some time passed, I reminded dad about the promised wagon and he assured me he would investigate further. Dad received new information that the council had changed our request from a wagon to a cart. My only question was: "How many wheels has a cart?" On hearing it had two wheels, I tried to imagine what such a cart would look like. Time passed and still no cart turned up. "Dad what is happening to the cart?" I asked. Dad again asked the council and they said that the cart "turned out to be an error".

I could not understand so I asked: "How many wheels has an error?" Mum and dad could not help but laugh and then explained what an error meant. From that time through decades in our lives "how many wheels has an error" established itself in the family as a standard saying when something was in doubt.

As a matter of fact, the council could not provide neither a wagon nor a cart. The wagon which mum pulled with me to Neuenburg owed its existence to our own initiative – we made it ourselves. On one of these shopping excursions mum managed to get a number of hot fresh bread loaves. On our way back home I could not resist the temptation to try this fresh smelling warm bread. When mum arrived home, she could not believe what had happened to our bread. I sat still, starring at mum – no bread was left. But the worst thing was that I felt terribly bad in my puffed-up stomach and it did not take long for me to throw up. Mum complained not only about the loss of the bread, but that it should have stayed in my stomach and served at least some purpose!

In front of our house stood a smaller house, where another family lived with one boy of my own age. The grandmother also lived in this house and she was very keen to keep her grandson, Roland, in impeccable condition. His hair was always thoroughly combed back and fixed with shiny pomade. As we played together enjoying real boyish pranks, there was always a big fuss at the end of a day at Roland's house because of his untidy condition. In contrast to Roland, I had my hair cut completely short. After each new haircut, that took place either at home or occasionally at the barber's in Neuenburg, I was angry when the other kids rubbed their hands over my short hair. One day I decided to lure Roland into a haircut with me. Somehow I managed to convince mum to give the additional 50 pfennig required for Roland's haircut.

Roland walked with me to the barber's in Neuenburg. It was my turn first to receive the usual haircut – right to the skin. When Roland's turn came, I instructed the barber to do the same, because I had paid beforehand. Roland could say nothing; his hair cut started and his long black pomade-shiny hair fell freely on the floor of the barber's shop. Roland looked very different after this haircut. His head looked so much smaller without his thick crop of hair. He definitely was not sure anymore, if he had done the right thing.

It became crystal clear at home that it wasn't the right thing to do. His grandma looked out of the kitchen window just when we arrived. She looked at me, looked at the other person, and looked at me again. Without doubt a storm was brewing. I realised it was time to leave this scene quickly. When grandma realised she was looking at Roland, she held her hands around her head crying: "Poor Roland, what have they done to you?" The grandma nearly fell through the window frame she became that excited. Roland was not allowed to see me anymore after this incident. He remained locked in the house and stayed away from school until his hair had grown halfway back.

To be honest, I was not really happy with that outcome. Roland's family took this event too seriously. All I had wanted was for Roland and I to appear at school with the same haircut and thus I would not receive the same attention I always got from the other kids.

School could not be ignored during that time. The nearest school to our place was in Rotenbach. A lady teacher, Ms Nothwang, lived in that building located at the entrance of this small village. Walking the two kilometres from home to school did not represent any problem. The school path crossed over a small bridge, which straddled the factory channel and followed the railway line. The railway station was just before the school.

Only a small number of students visited this school. All classes were in one room. Ms Nothwang was the only teacher and she addressed each class at a time. No student felt neglected. It seemed, this mixture of different class levels stimulated the learning process of the lower classes. Besides their own subjects, every student came in contact with the subjects of other classes. This did not create confusion, rather it opened the mind of each student.

The younger students looked up to the older students as they also wanted to reach their level of knowledge. A natural competition took place. Ms Nothwang demonstrated without question her authority in a gentle, but determined way. Discipline allowed this school system to function. The time after the war did not allow any other option, therefore the school operated well.

Despite all these positive attributes of this school, I performed only on an average level with the exception of music. My life at Geeswell Meadows was filled with lots of activities and I became sidetracked from my schoolwork. Educational priorities were not on my mind at the time. Ms Nothwang must have realised my difficulty in concentrating at school. She did not point out my weaknesses, but encouraged my musical talent. She offered that I could stay back after school to practice on her flute if she was happy with my day's performance. Extending my time at school restricted my activities at home, which were largely boy's pranks. I had a lot of respect for my teacher like all the other students in this school. Ms Nothwang was the first of a few outstanding teachers as I would experience later in my life. Her heart was simply with her pupils, therefore her pupils responded well to her teaching.

The simple solutions in life are always the difficult ones, which also applies in teaching.

Leaving home for school in the early hours of the morning became more of a regular event than returning home. There was always something to explore on the way home such as fish in the channel. I spent some time finding out how to catch a trout with my hand. I crouched on my knees at the riverbank, my hand motionless at the entrance of an underwater cave.

Waiting and watching with patience brought from time to time a trout out of its hiding place. As quick as lightning I had to throw the trout out of the water on to the land. I learned how slippery and strong the fish was after it escaped back into the water. To bring a nice-sized trout home made me proud. The catch didn't only become a welcome addition on our table, dad also remunerated me with a small amount of pocket money.

Coming home late on such occasions, I was told not to neglect any school duties. Doing my homework in the evenings was not my greatest strength and this didn't help much my school marks.

In this Geeswell Meadows' world many things attracted my attention.

Although there appeared not much to do, a lot of activities could be created here. Memories returned from Weilderstadt with my first attempts to raise a kite into the sky again. On a Saturday morning with mum's help the kite could make its first tests. Running with enthusiasm up the stone road I gradually released the line so that the kite could gain height. Not watching my steps, I fell and badly injured my left knee. Surgery was not available so all a doctor could do was clean the wound, disinfect it and give me a tetanus needle. This knee injury played up most of the time during my life, especially before a weather change. I quickly forgot about flying kites and concentrated instead on learning how to live with such a handicap which I actually did control over the years. My body was still young enough to compensate and rebuild this knee area. The ability to turn a disability into an ability played a vital role in my future life. In many cases we are only as sick as we think we are.

As planned, before one full calendar year passed, dad managed to get the factory floor ready to supply mechanical pulp to Weissenstein. To complete this job, Dad had to be innovative with incredible improvisations. The place had been badly dismantled by the Allied Forces. I did not understand much about technical requirements at the age of seven, but could relate to the long hours dad had sacrificed in his task. Nothing was available, everything had to be created out of primitive materials. Dad did an outstanding job. There wasn't even any power to the factory, the remaining installation was brutally wrecked.

Dad gained finally the upper hand. During the day the operation of the factory became evident only through the level of noise emanating from the building.

Nobody complained about the noise in the house. This operation provided work for a number of other people. In the beginning dad was preoccupied with fixing problems, when something went wrong. It took dad a while to find somebody, who could assist him in the task of keeping the place running.

One our family's first bonuses came out of this mammoth task, dad received a NSU motorcycle to travel between Rotenbach and Weissenstein. A motorcycle in those days represented quite an achievement. While other people could only dream about such a thing, Dr Heller again made this possible. According to dad's reports, Dr Heller was a genius in connecting to the right people in order to achieve his goals.

One weekend Dad sorted out timber planks on the factory floor. As I arrived on the platform of the stairway down to the factory, he asked me to hand him a nail lever. Instead of walking down the stairs, I made a shortcut and jumped down to the floor with the lever in my hand. A timber plank with a rusty big nail sticking up was waiting for my left foot. From the height I jumped, a nail forced itself right through my foot. Dad pulled the plank with the nail straight out of my foot. Another medical emergency developed because of my behaviour. Boyish pranks are the hard way to learn. In any case, luck was on my side because this happened on a weekend when dad was at home with his motorcycle. He quickly took me to a doctor in Pforzheim. The pain in my foot from this accident didn't go away quickly and for a number of years I was reminded of this incident.

One mishap rarely comes alone, the next one waited around the corner. There were wooden logs stored around our place for the factory. I wanted to use them to build a cubbyhouse.

Roland, my neighbourhood friend, showed his interest in the project and helped me begin building the cubbyhouse during our school holidays. One day Roland had left, but I stayed on keen to finish one of the corner posts. To hurry up, I swung my reversed axe to knock the post into the ground. But I swung too hard and the reversed axe ended up stuck in my head. A typical case of 'more haste, less speed'.

I rushed to the house for help. Mum yelled: "Martin, what have you done?" Another emergency. Dad tied me up on the motorcycle, my head was covered in towel bandages with the axe still in place. It was confirmed in the hospital that I would not have survived if the axe had been removed before I got to hospital.

Luck was on my side and again I had learned a painful lesson. These kind of pranks had to stop! As a result, the cubbyhouse remained in an unfinished state.

The situation throughout the country had not changed much.

However changes in our life were significant. More time could be allocated to make ourselves more comfortable in home as we had a little bit more money. The preferred deal still was the exchange of goods and one valuable item from Geeswell Meadows was honey. A beekeeper started to set up bee populations collecting honey from the surrounding Black Forest fir trees. This dark honey is famous for its taste, a taste only the Black Forest can supply.

In Spring time, when the Black Forest released this honey, the bees busily spent all day collecting it and bringing it to their beehive to feed their queen bee and store the excess in frames filled with bees wax cells. These beehives attracted my curiosity. Nobody had to tell me that bees demand respect – their bites cannot be ignored. When the time was right to collect the honey, we were allowed to assist with our neighbours. Mr Breitling, the beekeeper, was the only person allowed to enter the shed which housed a large number of beehives. He wore full protective clothing and had a dense net over his head and across his shoulders. His hands were covered with cotton gloves. Mr Breitling explained that he moved very slowly from the far end of the beehive and opened one top lid after the other to access the frames where the honey wax cells were fully loaded. The bees that flew out of the box followed him and the honey frames. He had to keep his movements, particularly his hand movements, slow and steady to ensure the bees also followed slowly. Mr Breitling could control the bees this way. If, for some reason, there was a sudden movement, the bees acted immediately and more bees joined the swarm. Mr Breitling told us that the bees knew him quite well and even trusted him despite being deprived of their honey and receiving only sugar in return. This is not the only occasion where we 'cheat' to gain an advantage over nature.

The white protective clothing helped the bees recognise Mr Breitling. Their beehives were also white with coloured stripes on each of the boxes to identify them. The bees didn't need the coloured stripes, they knew their box by other means. Some bees would stand guard at the entrance of each box to make sure the right bees entered the right box.

Now, back to the honey-winning process. The frame with the honeycombs was placed in the centrifuge kettle. With the lid firmly closed, a handle moved the kettle around and this centrifugal force removed the honey from the combs. The honey ran down the inner wall of the kettle and a golden, shiny tin collected this nectar.

It took all the day to complete all the boxes. With daylight disappearing the bees had to be left alone. Without daylight, the bees became confused and could not settle in their boxes.

Mr Breitling knew his bees quite well, but could not prevent some bees following him into the centrifuge room while delivering the honeycomb frames. Sometimes we would get stung during this process. Mr Breitling had a list to keep a tally of who got stung. Those with the most 'ticks' were duly compensated in honey at the end of the day. This must have been a good honey year as many large tin containers were stacked up in Mr Breitling's truck. For our assistance with the centrifuge, mum and myself received a good share of the honey. Such quality honey was a very valuable exchange item in those days.

Soon after the honey harvest, the first fruits began ripening in a cherry tree near the beehives on Mr Breitling's property. The dark red cherries certainly attracted my attention. The tree was fully loaded with more cherries than anybody could eat and were just asking to be picked. I enlisted the help of the neighbour's son, Roland. To reach the cherries more easily, I had to climb up the centre of the tree. Roland remained on the ground. What we did not see was a huge formation of bees hanging on to their queen in the middle of the tree. When I climbed the tree, the bees decided to defeat the 'intruder'. I could not have come down the tree fast enough. Even when I had my feet on the ground and ran towards the house, the swarm of bees followed me.

Mum did not have to ask what had happened. For hours she sat next to my bed pulling out hundreds of stings from my legs, arms and head. As a consequence, I found myself in a state of delirium for days – the fever sent me into another world. All the food abandoned my stomach, cold compresses were the only medicine available.

In writing this many years later, I do not know how I survived this bee experience! But something good did come out of the bee attack – my body should be immune to rheumatism for the rest of my life.

Mum and dad informed Mr Breitling about the incident and he quickly came over, dressed in full protective gear, to catch these bees. He gave me a nice big tin of honey to help me get through this dreadful experience.

Dad's success with the factory brought more stability into our lives. The initial necessity to make everything ourselves eased. More money and time became available for goods and pursuits that were not on a list of necessities.

Mum's hobby was making puppets and she would perform shows with these puppets in our home. When a special occasion, like my birthday, came up our living room was transformed into a theatre. Some 20 children from the neighbourhood, school and town came to my home to enjoy a fantastic play. From primitive materials, Mum created a clown, a policeman, a donkey – and with each performance she added a new character. Mum invented the scenes herself. Her fingers moved the puppets skillfully. So good was she at this puppet show that her young audience was under the impression she was not behind the scene.

A board between the door frame served as the scenery. The puppets were displayed through a window in this board which was framed by curtains. Once the curtains opened, mum encouraged the audience to join her dialogue – to keep everybody's attention high. How could she handle more than two puppets with only two hands? Only after a show did I find that a number of puppets were attached on strings, which mum moved skillfully with one or both legs, if necessary.

An afternoon being entertained by mum's puppet show became a special occasion on the calendar. Each show became a success, stimulating the minds of the young audience and the fantasy continued on in each child's memory. I won many new friends through these puppet shows.

Winter 1947-1948 brought a lot of snow to our area. When Christmas came closer, dad took me into the snow-covered forest to collect a fir tree for our Christmas. Dad received the permission from the local forestry to cut one small tree out of the forest. We were on foot, the deep snow making our excursion a slow one. On our way back home, nightfall caught up with us under a clear, starry sky and moonshine. The scent of our fresh fir tree, the darkness in the forest, the lights out of the sky reflected on an open, white snowfield is forever etched in my memory. Dad and I stepped through the deep snowfields down towards our valley. The night air was freezing cold, warm breath 'steamed' out of our mouths with every step. Christmas preparations could not have been better.

This tree shined on Christmas Eve with its wax candles looking like the moon and the stars in the Black Forest.

This severe winter made it difficult to run the factory in the ground floor of the house. Ice blocked the water wheel in the channel. The cold weather made work with machines and water very difficult. During that winter, life became a struggle. When the cold receded, sudden mild temperatures brought heavy rain in early March.

Layers of snow disappeared with the rain in a matter of hours. The rain became a deluge and we were trapped in our house for almost a week by the swollen river, which filled the entire valley including the road on the north side and the railway line in the south. Our home became surrounded by constant rushing water. When we looked out of a window from our second floor, the vast sea of floodwater was a frightening sight. Debris flowed down the river, which remained at a high water level even after the rains had stopped after a few days. Then one morning the sun shone brightly in the sky, promising good weather again. I looked out of the window to the north, where the neighbour's house stood. What a surprise – the receding waters had dug a big hole between the two houses. Luckily our house had deep foundations strong enough to withstand such water currents. What would we have done, if our house had washed away? This situation was impossible to think of, there would have been no way to escape from the force of these torrents.

Our cellar, where we stored potatoes, apples, and preserving jars, was on the factory level. During the floods, the wooden door to the cellar became so swollen with water that we could not open it. When the waters finally receded, and the door shrunk back to its original size, we could finally survey the damage. Dad was the first to enter the cellar. All the potatoes and apples floated right under the ceiling. But with the door open, the water rushed out of the cellar taking all the potatoes and apples. Our food stores were flushed into the factory channel. Nobody could keep the door closed against the water pressure from inside. By the time we could close the door, almost nothing was left.

The water damage in the factory was enormous. Only with massive help from the factory workers in Weissenstein was it possible to get the place running again in a relatively short time. Our lives had to get restarted out of ruins during the summer of 1948.

One day I went with dad on his motorbike to the factory in Weissenstein. On our way we passed what remained of the city of Pforzheim which was bombed relentlessly just before the end of the war. What I saw exceeded all my imaginings.

The entire city was flattened, but a rebuilding process had started. People had cleared passages in the rubble by hand. I could not see over the top of these rubble passages. Finding ourselves in a labyrinth, Dad had to ask a number of people for directions to find our way around the city. The railway station near the town centre looked bizarre. Not only were the buildings just rubble, but railway lines with carriages were piled up high into the sky. An intense battle had taken place around this railway station. A small pocket of resistance from the German army put up a ferocious battle here with the Allied Forces. The German soldiers were hiding under the wheel axles of the many railway carriages stationed here. While the Allied Forces tried to systematically destroy the carriages, they met untold resistance which inflicted heavy casualties on the Allied side. When the Allies realised where the resistance was coming from, they turned their sheer military force on the city and its railway station. An untold number of civilians died in bomb raids during the nights just before the end of the war.

We came out of Pforzheim and continued our trip to one of its outer suburbs, Weissenstein. In contrast to Pforzheim, Weissenstein was spared the bombardment.

The factory in Weissenstein was also much larger than the one at Geeswell Meadows.

The factory's entrance had a guard in uniform who took dad's details and went back into his control room. After returning, he opened the gate and asked us to follow him. Dr Heller welcomed us into his office. He stood up from behind his shiny desk and came towards us with both his hands ready to shake ours. Each of us was offered a seat at a table. My attention was quickly fixed on a round blue 'ball' mounted on a timber stand. While dad and Mr Heller started talking, I moved closer to this 'ball' and discovered that it revolved on an axis. Moments later, dad said to me: "This ball represents our planet Earth." I became fascinated, a lot of things went through my mind at the same time. Dr Heller explained: "We are standing right here now, everything is just reduced in size. The 'ball' is rotating very evenly under the watchful eye of our sun, its contours show land masses in a vast blue ocean."

Then he said: "Soon I will go to America by boat". And he traced the route on the globe with his finger.

Then we were served a drink and a sandwich, which was much appreciated. After that, we visited the factory. Big rolls covered in steam showed a long assembly with white paper. It was very noisy. I did not understand much of what happened here.

After our factory tour, we were invited to dinner in town. I enjoyed the comfortable ride in a motor car; everybody had his own seat and could close his own door. A motorbike seat was quite different from this. As the end of this day drew closer, it was time to go home. Dad explained to me that the meeting with Mr Heller was very important. "Our next home and a new job for me will be here in Weissenstein, as soon as somebody else can take over Geeswell Meadows," dad said.

A new task awaited dad in Weissenstein. He split his days between Geeswell Meadows and Weissenstein for the next few months and worked long hours.

Settlement Weissenstein

Everything started to change in the autumn of 1949, when all our belongings were picked up by a truck and moved to our new home in Weissenstein. I could not say goodbye to the friendly old lady living in the house with us because she had gone. One day men entered her rooms, carried her away and she was never seen again.

Our new home in Weissenstein looked more like a villa, high up from the road leading to the factory gate.

The rooms were much smaller. On the floor above us lived other people. Everything seemed to be better, but also quite different. A room with a bath, a gas boiler for hot water, a wash basin, toilet, wall mirror and towel racks became a new experience for me. There was no excuse anymore to have a 'cat wash'.

Life continued quite peacefully in this new place. There were many more children at the local school. Each class had its own room and my class had more students than all the classes in Rotenbach. We had different teachers for different subjects – this was all a new experience for me. I attended school as required, but still had little interest in learning. For a while I missed my friends and the school at Rotenbach. But time helped to heal the 'young wounds' and soon I became comfortable with my new life in Weissenstein and its daily routine.

Next to my new house there was a chicken yard which was home to a few hens and a colourful rooster. Mum did the daily feeding and I did my best to keep this place clean. It never became evident whether the chooks appreciated my cleaning efforts or not. I tried to establish a relationship with them without success. They never responded the way I thought.

Are chickens dumb? They move for food, they retreat with sudden fear. It is either peace or a battle when the rooster tried to establish his authority. Only one thing was for sure, the hens laid the eggs which was obviously the purpose of their existence.

A chook's face will never tell you if it is happy or sad – the face is always unchanged. Only their movements give an indication of the chook's mood.

When my duties with the chooks were at an end, my attention focused on the forest on the hill next to us. For hours I walked the rocky slopes looking out for a deer, a hare or birds in the trees. On a hot summer's day, not far from our place, was a public swimming pool in the open which offered a retreat and a chance to catch up with my class mates.

The water in the pool was much warmer than that of river Enz. It also irritated my eyes, so I decided not to fully submerge in this water.

The first winter here also brought plenty of snow and so the sledge replaced the swimming shorts. Only few children owned a sledge at that time so it became quite common for children to share their sledges. Instead of heading home straight after school, I played in the snow. Time went so quickly, nobody realised it. When these winter games finally stopped at the end of a day, I got usually very late home. No time was left to do homework for the next day. The welcome at home was very predictable: the question arose, was the fun after school worth it?

Winter doesn't last forever. Easter turned up on the calendar with a change of season. It was a tradition to have an Easter egg hunt outside the house. One Easter, I was keen to search outside the house to see what the Easter Bunny might have left for me. The small garden in front of my house did not require much of an effort to search. What I found appeared to be very little for me, so I extended my search past our garden. I could not believe what I found across the road: the Easter bunny had left so much that I could not collect them all in one go. I was full of joy. But mum and dad became worried as to where all these Easter presents came from. I had to show them the place of this rich discovery. Dad had the answer immediately for me: "You are on the neighbour's property, the Easter bunny left this for the neighbour's children. You have to return them." But I was the one, who found all this. Why did I have to return it to somebody else? I regarded myself as a winner in the search for Easter eggs.

But my opinion did not matter. The neighbour's children came and I had to give them their Easter eggs.

The children, two boys and a girl, must have enjoyed their role, receiving their Easter eggs without any effort. On the other hand, I was not a happy boy losing all these eggs with the stroke of a word and not receiving anything in return for my efforts. This Easter became a disappointment for me.

But this event quickly lost its significance because other things happened as well: Dr Heller had died during his trip to America. According to eye witnesses, Dr Heller dived from the ship into the ocean and was never seen again. His death was to change our lives dramatically. The situation at the Weissenstein factory changed immediately, as if a number of people were waiting for such incident to happen.

Rational thinking was replaced with politics and dad became the first one to be exposed to such moves within the factory. Somebody must have disliked the fact that dad had joined the management team thanks to Dr Heller.

Achievements didn't seem to count anymore and dad decided to move on and leave Weissenstein.

We had clocked just one year there, when this happened. Dad immediately found another appointment in a paper manufacturing company in the town of Ettlingen, near Karlsruhe. For the first couple of months, dad came home only on weekends. Mum and I still continued to live in Weissenstein. The day to move could not come soon enough, our lives became more and more disrupted and somebody else was after the rooms in which we lived.

Settlement Ettlingen

The new home in Ettlingen stood on factory property. We occupied the first floor and the rooms were larger than in Weissenstein. I had even a room of my own. For a number of years, Ettlingen became an important place in our lives. I started to go out into the world from there, whereas for mum and dad, Ettlingen became the last destination in their lives.

It was 1951 when we moved to Ettlingen. My enrolment at the local school was one of our first priorities. The school was built in solid rock like most schools at the end of the 18th century and was just opposite the historic wall of the ancient town. Class four, which I attended, was on the ground floor at the corner of the building. This was a good location for the times when I was late for school. I could just sneak unseen into the class through a window.

This period was also a time when everything in education was constantly changed – the start of the school year, subjects and teachers. It appeared that somebody in the Education Ministry wanted to leave his mark behind in history.

Everybody started to learn English the year I joined primary school in year four. Within one year the subject was taken off the list – a decision with no positive outcome. Primary school was downgraded at the expense of the next 'higher' level of school – the 'Gymnasium'.

Mum and dad decided that at the end of year four, I should attend entry exams to the Gymnasium. I made this entry to my parents' satisfaction but did not understand, at that time, the importance of that achievement. My parents 'wrapped up my future' in their way but I could not really honour this vocation by becoming the 'good student' Martin. Teachers gave me two chances to repeat a class and nobody was happy about that. I could not develop the expected interest for school. Any complaint from school was met at home with heavy disciplinary measures. My parents failed to express their wishes and I didn't know what I wanted – they never asked me. Dad had to deal with a lot of problems in the factory of Ettlingen. He was expected to be the undisputed boss at home and mum tried hard to keep the peace most of the time with patience and understanding.

One day, mum's youngest sister moved with her little daughter, Constance, into the ground floor of our house. This happened on an understanding of helping each other. We could steadily improve our lives financially through dad's work.

Constance was four years younger than I so she played somewhat the role of a sister for me. This proved to be good although she was not with us all the time, living downstairs with her mum. There was not enough time for even a quarrel between us.

School holidays are welcome breaks for everybody – teachers, students, parents. One set of holidays, dad decided on a road trip. We first drove in our newly-acquired Volkswagen to Weilderstadt. When time would allow, we also planned to see Rotenbach and on the way home Weissenstein, a nostalgic journey back in time. The atmosphere was great and instead of staying at home or going to school, we went back to where we started. The farmhouse of the Borger family remained exactly the same way we had left it. Mum couldn't help but say to Mrs Borger: "What have you got?" This was a common greeting that people asked to exchange goods, when no money was around after the war.

Going back to our past showed us how far we had come. We had reason to be proud. Mum and dad were again on track. In Weilderstadt, mum stood up to very different conditions. She did what had to be done to survive and this, without doubt, was a remarkable credit for mum.

On another holiday it was decided to reunite with family members. We met dad's sister, Kathy, and her family in a small place called Almandle, where she and her three children had spent the past two weeks with a farmer's family.

We stayed at the farmer's place and helped to bring in the hay on that weekend. The summer day was hot and a picnic on the field was arranged – a very welcome break for everybody. Working with hay in fresh air created a good appetite, especially for the younger generation. Hunger was still the ' best cook ', even a piece of bread tasted wonderful. The farmer's family contributed their own cider which everybody enjoyed. Towards the end of this day, just before dusk, everybody moved back to the farm on top of the fully-loaded hay wagon. The farmer pulled his hay with a tractor – this wagon moved very differently from the one in Weilderstadt with the galloping horse in front! The tractor arrived with its load of hay in front of the barn gate. Everybody was told to move away from the top of the hay wagon as the arch of the gate allowed just the hay to pass under. Everybody else got off the hay wagon in time except me.

All of a sudden the tractor moved again, pulling the hay wagon into the barn. This happened so quickly that I hit the arch of the gate and was pushed off the hay, ending up with my back on one side of an arch stone used to keep the wheels away from the arch sides. No matter how hard I tried, my breath stopped. For how long, I can't remember. It took a while until somebody saw me struggling for my breath. My face must have shown all sorts of colours. I also could not get up with my back pain. An angel must have decided: "This is enough suffering, here is your breathing back ". Suddenly I could breath again, but the pain in my back remained. Nobody even thought to have my back examined because, with my breath back ' I tried my best to carry on like everybody else. Our short holiday drew to an end and we had to return to Ettlingen. This failure to pay appropriate attention to my back caught up with me later in an awkward way.

Let me first continue with every day life after this weekend farming experience.

I must admit to being not too keen on going back to school. Looking back on school life, poses some questions. I am not questioning the teaching authority and I know there were students doing well at school. In the teaching culture there are still elements which I'd like to highlight. Today, when I write about this, I have gained some distance and so look back with some humour, but also with criticism. A view without a critical substance is of no value. The number of teachers I met during my school life was exceptionally high. Every new teacher tried to do his best working with the process of a formal education. Teachers' contributions should be recognised as a basis for a student to deal with life situations after school. I remember one outstanding teacher, who broadened his discussion past the formal education guidelines by questioning the fact that teachers have a limited time to become prepared for the job in front of a class.

He suggested that they should go out into the real world to learn what life expects from students after school.

Teaching institutions and the real world have always been miles apart. A lot of teachers have never left the school bench. They are looking at the world from their secure environment which society has provided. Some people even have the opinion that "if you can't do it, teach it". Teachers should be regarded at the top of society – they are participating in the responsibility of preparing a new generation. The focus on formal education is a necessity, but not a priority! A teacher's personality decisively determines the outcome of an education. There were teachers whose authority never became an issue, others invited an alerted youth into undisciplined behaviour. How should a class react to an outburst from a teacher such as this: "Who doesn't believe in God, must leave the class room".

Teachers are also human beings and no human being is perfect. But in their role, teachers are highly exposed and caution is a priority. It is by no means a school that determines the outcome in a life. It can be regarded only as a contribution to somebody's own efforts in life. Don't let us forget that the real school is life! And for that reason we are bound to learn as long as we live. School does not release us from the task to keep learning for the rest of our lives. It can be understood, therefore, why good school performers are not necessarily good achievers in life. The medium school performers seem to become the better achievers. A common observation, when a class reunion takes place after many years.

Life Improves – School Years

Boy scouts and music

After my school days, the local boy scouts movement attracted more and more of my attention. Also in the late 1950s television started to enter everybody's home. The local cinema was one of the few entertainments before television. Cinema wasn't a daily event, however, because of long working hours and little money.

The boy-scout movement in our town represented an opportunity for young people to learn to live closer to nature.

We regularly attended Saturday afternoon boy scout meetings with school friends.

I was lucky to have an excellent leader. His example made a lasting impression on all of us. We met in our own hut and prepared for yearly boy scouts events. Hobby constructions out of a variety of materials promoted skills in a team environment – we worked mostly in small groups. Tools were not an issue. The task was to create something useful with minimum expense. Singing became also a regular event with a guitar supplying the musical support.

Hildegard guides young musicians, Martin and Constance

The nearby forests and hills of the Black Forest offered vast opportunities for hiking and tracking. One group, for instance, set signs made from branches on a track and we had to follow these signs. The tasks were often outlined with a time frame. Performing well in these tasks was a major goal. A physically fit and good observer in nature had the best chances to win. The position of the sun, the moon and the stars at night; recognising the wet mossy sides of tree trunks; identifying wildlife tracks; memorising identification points like a tree, a quarry or a far point on the horizon – all such elements made for good observation skills. Our time outdoors provided us also with exercises to learn to live off nature without interfering with its sensitive balance. Which berries grew in our forests and what time of the year did they ripen? Dandelions and young stinging nettles cooked in a pot could supply a nutritious soup.

A boy scout in his uniform should always carry with him a knife, matches and string. If he was on a mission, he should carry a basic first-aid kit. First aid was an important part of our training and our skills had to be renewed every now and then.

It was a very strict procedure to arrange a safe fireplace in the open for cooking purposes and only wood from the ground should be used. To stay overnight with appropriate permission in an outdoor place, boy scouts carried in their backpacks parts for a tent. We called this tent a ' jurte' which originated from Mongolia. The centre of a tent can be kept open so that a fire could be built inside, contained by a ring of stones, and the smoke released through the top of the tent. A boy scout must be in the position to start a controlled fire – no matter what the circumstances were – whether it was wet or the supply of fire materials was short. Even horse manure could be used for a fire. A fireplace was never left alone. When a fire was finished, the glowing ashes had to be covered completely with stones and clean soil. If a fire was maintained during night, one person was always in charge of guarding the fire, whether it was outside or inside the tent.

All boy scout groups were united in a 'family' and the families formed an 'aerie'. The boy scout movement in Ettlingen had a patron, who substantially sponsored our group. Our patron, Theo Zurstrassen, made available his block of land outside town for monthly meetings with all boy scout groups. These meetings became a memorable event for many years. Theo opened each meeting with an inauguration speech. Then followed activity reports from individual groups, group plans, presentations, plays and songs plus instrumental performances.

Our group embarked more and more on songs accompanied by guitars. One person in our group, Bernhard, stood out as a particularly talented musician. He encouraged others to participate and to constantly lift our level of performance. Training sessions were set up during our own meetings and we also practiced at home. Performance in music gained a foothold in everybody's life and we all enjoyed this.

When we performed for a special event, we enjoyed presenting a special madrigal from time to time.

My mum became aware of my love for music. I joined the Music Conservatory in Karlsruhe, where I regularly practiced in a quartet of recorders. I still remember our teacher Mr Wehrle, a musician 'par-excellence'. This elderly music professor usually appeared with a low profile. Dressed in his characteristic felt coat, he was passionate about his music. He mastered a number of instruments encouraging us to follow his example. His favourite instrument was the zither which he only played on very special occasions and when he was happy with our progress. We listened to these performances in complete silence, such was our respect for this musician.

I extended my interest in music to a guitar and soon to an accordion. A piano was out of reach that time.

Meanwhile, dad became unsettled about my ambitions in music. He believed I was spending too much time on music and ordered me to stop music completely and to concentrate on my schoolwork. I was determined not to abandon my guitar, at least, and I kept playing this unnoticed for some time.

It was during this period that an incident with a co-tenant of my house had a far-reaching impact on my life. John, a high-profile actor, fell sick with open tuberculosis. He had to undergo surgery and one of his lungs was completely removed. Unfortunately, I also fell sick.

Hospital

I was diagnosed with tuberculosis and was immediately isolated and transferred to a special clinic in Friedenweiler, which was located in the southern part of the Black Forest. I personally did not feel that bad, therefore I could not understand the rush. I had nothing to say but to follow the procedures at the big hospital.

My time spent in Friedenweiler became a turning point in my life. I did not have to ask about the disease as I saw with my own eyes patients of various age groups trapped in ill health for the rest of their lives. I was determined not to spend my life there. Fortunately, a doctor, Mrs Dischinger, a woman of outstanding character, helped me a lot through this ordeal. As well as tuberculosis, I also developed major back problems. As I was kept in a bed in isolation, and therefore had little movement, my old back problem flared up again. I could not move in bed and would not even wish my worst enemy this pain. The clinical staff became aware of my handicap and examinations resulted in a plaster around my entire body.

Every morning I had a visit from this lady doctor. I began looking forward to this visit, because Mrs Dischinger was the only person coming to see me and supporting my writing efforts. My subjects were of a diverse nature. On each visit Mrs Dischinger would ask me: "What has Martin written for me today?" She showed special interest towards my writing and spent time with me to discuss openly each day's work. I found it very worthwhile to fill in my time by writing. This way I could focus away from my situation – my mind transferred me into a world outside this clinical environment. For my own reasons I did not take part in discussions of other patients' conditions, as I was determined not to stay here for long.

Mum and dad came with other family members to see me. They knew how bad my situation was, far more than I was prepared to admit. Everybody seemed to focus on the bad side, demonstrating their sympathy. I asked myself: "Who is the sick person here?"

Life went on unchanged for nearly one year. Every day, I received antibiotic injections, which I really started to hate. Not only did they hurt, but they had very unpleasant side effects on my bowel movements. With the discovery of penicillin, a large number of medical conditions were treated with that drug at that time, with little knowledge of its side effects. Somehow I survived this treatment. As I remained in constant discussion with Mrs Dischinger about my condition, we agreed to abandon my plaster just before one year.

The itchy irritation under the plaster had become intolerable. Finally the day arrived when the plaster was cut off. After a thorough cleaning, I initially felt much better. But only then I learned that I was unable to move or even try to take a step. With auxiliary equipment, I had to learn to walk again like a baby. In the first days, my progress was hardly visible, but then my body started to progressively regain strength.

Mrs Dischinger developed a specific set of bed gymnastics to support my recovery. I worked very hard on these exercises, and still continue them to this day. The success of these exercises begged the question, whether I should have been put in a plaster cast at all.

Finally, I felt I was ready to leave Friedenweiler Sanatorium. Mrs Dischinger urged me to be cautious and not jeopardize, what we had achieved so far. I had to put on weight and gain more stability, before I could be discharged especially in regard to my past tuberculosis condition. Coming so close to a promising freedom into a 'normal world', I was determined to increase my weight. I used all imaginable tricks and even put weights into my pyjama pockets when it was time to check on my weight gain.

I still spent Christmas 1954 in Friedenweiler. I had managed to walk freely by then – but only for a short time, because my body very quickly became exhausted. That Christmas in Friedenweiler became a very memorable time for me. Because of my love for music, I was delighted to have the leading role in a play which was held in the hospital's function hall with all patients and staff present. I freed myself to perform in front of all other patients forgetting completely that I was also one of them, but not for much longer.

Early January the day arrived when I left Friedenweiler. It was a quiet occasion.

I had time enough to contemplate the situations of other patients, who were in Friedenweiler mainly because of their smoking habits. There were serious cases – patients who had no hope ever leaving this place. This experience strengthened my determination to never smoke or willingly harm my own health. Health is partly given to us, but we are responsible in looking after it and building on it. We all could be healthier and happier if we only comprehended the importance of taking responsibility for our own health. Some people only comprehend this when it is too late.

I left Friedenweiler on a sunny winter's day with a heavy snow layer over the Black Forest. Dad and mum picked me up with the car. The snow on the road meant we had to drive carefully. As soon as we left the higher region of the Black Forest, the snow disappeared and we could drive home without delay.

I could attend school immediately at the same year level that I had left one year ago. At home and around I looked at familiar things from a different angle after been away over one year. I realised only then, how beautiful many things were. Life returned slowly to normal. I could practice music again, join the family of boy scouts and I also slowly started to take up sports. The problem with my back did not disappear. From time to time I had to struggle to get over it. Under no circumstances did I want to go back to Friedenweiler and for that reason I willingly ignored doctors. Soon I realised that sports helped me to rebuild my strength. A meeting with my sports teacher revealed that he also lived with a severe back problem which he suffered after being buried alive by a shell during the war. Years of unsuccessful treatments followed until he decided to take the matter into his own hands by enjoying an active life with gymnastics, swimming, maximum activities and a healthy lifestyle.

Mr Kary, the sports teacher, was living proof of the value of sports and a positive attitude. He developed into an outstanding athlete with a dedication to helping young people through a broad range of sports activities.

Sports

'The die was cast' here for my future and the rest of my life. I enjoyed specific daily gymnastics combined with controlled activities to manage my back problem.

A couple of years later I learned that climatic conditions also contributed to my back problem. This occurred in 1964 when I travelled with a friend in a canoe for six weeks through Southern France.

It was the first time that I experienced no back pain at all. I know there are a lot of people in this world that have a back problem for one or another reason. It might even sound trivial to discuss such a disabling condition in writing. I, however, maintain that it is worthwhile discussing a subject and sharing it with other people, even if they haven't experienced similar disabling conditions. We only can learn from one another, this ultimately is also the justification for writing.

Life for me continued in Ettlingen with home, school and sports events that took me to other places to compete. During these sports trips, I gained new friendships based on similar interests and I enjoyed this very much.

Life with the boy scout movement also continued. I filled my time with activities.

Mum and dad regarded this as a good thing in a young life, however they would have liked to see more efforts going into school. I did not exactly hate school, but I tried rather to survive with the least amount of effort. I also admit that I certainly was not an easy student for my teachers.

One day it was decided that cousin Fred from another branch of the family should come and join us in Ettlingen. Cousin Fred and I enjoyed each other's company. He was more of a quiet boy, slightly younger than me, but this did not stop him enjoying most of the activities which I undertook. At school, Fred was an average student like myself and this helped strengthen our friendship. The house in Ettlingen had a large garden which boasted a garden house with a table and benches. Many hours of work went into this garden in our spare time. The longer daylight in summer evenings allowed the whole family to meet for dinner in the garden house; everybody enjoyed such time at the end of a day.

A classmate, Oswin, lived with his parents in their factory. He had access to various machines and so we planned to build a rocket and launch it into the sky. As a launching place we agreed on the area in our garden. The rocket turned out as a masterpiece, thanks to the machining facilities in Oswin's factory. Then out of a 'mechano set' grew a platform.

One afternoon everything was ready for a launch. Our rocket was packed with black powder. It took a number of attempts to launch the rocket. We experienced a frightening situation that we will never forget: once our rocket reached the required temperature, it took off with an incredible bang. Our ears became totally blocked and nobody could hear anything for quite a while. The expulsion heat of the rocket momentarily blinded everybody around. This shock dampened our pride and joy. Mum appeared in the far window of the house and knew immediately that we had done something we shouldn't have. Even pedestrians on the road across the river were visibly shaken by the bang of our rocket. Several classmates mentioned the bang at school the next day.

All we three, Oswin, Fred and I, did learn a lesson from this experience. We all could have been easily killed. I kept the platform for a number of years – the force of the rocket blast had punched a hole right through the 6mm steel plate. Where our rocket went, nobody knew. No more rocket launches was the unanimous answer.

When I focus back on school, I have to admit that the company of my cousin Fred did not much help our performances. School was just a necessity in my view. It held nothing to inspire me. There were other students producing the kind of inspiration that teachers like to see. Discipline was an accepted fact in those years. Teachers demanded it and enforced it with disciplinary measures to keep a student longer in school and often the cane was used on students' hands to further enforce the rules. The use of the cane did not work. It is not much different from a dog receiving a lesson. If it is instant, a dog can relate to it and a message sinks in; if it is not instant, then a lesson will fail in its message. Finally, a cane from a teacher has never done damage to anybody. I know we think differently today. Have we achieved the required discipline a class requires? We have to work harder on discipline today than ever before.

The discipline I experienced in my school days could be classified as reasonable. A teacher's personality determined the method and success of maintaining discipline. I remember a fantastic example when a student lost his temper and said to the teacher: "Kiss my arse". The teacher simply turned this incident down and responded: "No, I don't intend to do it". And this was the end of it. Isn't this a superior way to deal with teenage problems?

Compared with life at home, school presented to students something new every day in many different ways. Very often, it is only after we have left school that we realise how good school times were and how much smaller problems were at that time.

Discipline in my home was applied in a strict way. Mum managed through her adaptability to ease situations from time to time. Dad enforced discipline the way he was taught by his family. For instance, when you eat at the table your arms have to be tight at your body. To learn this correctly once and for all, a book was placed under each armpit during dinner. Discipline became enforced. I could not easily accept these measures and at times I felt I was 'getting the cane' from everywhere – home and school.

First Journeys

Germany – Denmark

The summer school holidays brought a welcome break. Fred's parents convinced my parents to allow Fred and I to undertake a bicycle tour to the north of Germany and join his parents on a holiday. Even my parents agreed, mainly because of my boy scout experience. First we caught the train to the city of Hannover which was more than half the distance to Fred's parents home. Before beginning our bicycle tour, I wanted to say hello to a friend who had moved from our neighbourhood in Ettlingen to Hannover. This friend, Edward, meant a lot to me. Despite him being a few years older, we had a good time together. When we found Edward's new home we only met his mother. Edward was also away for holidays.

We spent the nights in youth hostels, if available. We rode our packed bicycles mainly through the heath of Luneburg towards the harbour city of Bremen. Pleasant summer weather and very little traffic on these country roads helped to make our tour a success. We stopped a few times before nightfall on farms, where we had to convince the farmers that we were not smokers and wouldn't attempt to start any fires. One night we were allowed to stay in a hay barn. It was here I heard for the first time a dialect called 'Platt Deutsch'. Numbers and a lot of words were exactly like English – an obvious relationship between our two countries. This flat country featured typical farmhouses made from red brick walls and thatched roofs. The people were friendly people even though they were reserved. This countryside with its colourful summer heath won our hearts.

Our next destination was Bremer-Hafen. Mum's brother lived there with his family. They welcomed us. We had a bed to sleep on for a change and food out of a kitchen. During our short stay we got to know this family and how hard they had worked to rebuild their lives after the war. The entire family lived under the same roof and everybody contributed to family life.

Time told us to move on. The city of Flensburg, the destination for a reunion with Fred's parents, lay far ahead in bicycle terms so some hard leg pushing still had to be done on our bicycles.

We bypassed the big city of Hamburg. A ferry boat took us to the other side of the river Elbe, just before the outskirts of Hamburg.

We passed Schleswig-Holstein with its green pastures and grazing black and white cattle. Windmills and canals gave us the impression of Holland. This last leg of our tour brought us quicker than we anticipated to Flensburg.

With a sunny sky above us for most of the time, our bicycle tour was a success.

In Flensburg I saw the Baltic Sea for the first time. Life for the next two weeks was spent mainly around a hut on the beach, way out of the city of Flensburg. We met also a local fisherman who supplied us daily with fresh fish. Fish with fresh potatoes and butter milk for a drink – we could not ask for a better meal at our beach location. The weather was exceptionally warm. We could swim in the warm water as long as we wanted. A small boat was organised so that Fred and I could catch our own fish. One time, we became caught by a freak storm. It was only then we remembered the local fisherman's warning: "A small ocean like the Baltic Sea can develop very quickly into choppy waves that are difficult to control with a small boat."

We just made it back to our place after a frightening battle with the elements of the sea.

A visit to the city of Flensburg became a change to our daily life on the beach. We had to dress ourselves properly for this occasion. A boating show of new luxury boats attracted a large number of people into town. The beautiful summer weather helped to create a relaxed atmosphere in this historic 'Hanse town'. On another day we took the train to nearby Denmark. People used to buy agricultural products across this border: milk, cheese, eggs and meat, because Denmark was much cheaper. The free movements of people across the border indicated that the two countries had good relations. I recognised the similarities in their languages and people didn't look much different on either side of the border. This became my first excursion into another country.

Our destination that day was the island of Sylt which stretches along the coast of the North Sea a short distance from the main-land. A stiff breeze blew all day from the sea, despite a sunny, blue sky above us. The wind kept the air noticeably cooler, the water of this restless ocean turned out even colder again. The powerful waves had also created a very different beach formation from the one on the Baltic Sea. High, long sand dunes met the waves here and the constant wind only allowed the grass to gain a foothold in protected areas.

Our day on the island of Sylt became a long one for all of us. All that wind, the fresh sea air and the cold water of the North Sea certainly built up an appetite. Which was greater, the appetite or the fatigue, nobody really knew. The main issue became getting back after such a long and eventful day.

Like everything that comes to an end, this holiday did the same. It afforded far-reaching gains: new impressions in new places, new people, new challenges. All this prepares us better for our lives.

It wasn't long after this holiday that disillusionment set in as school days took over daily life again. We need to learn. Life is like a long distance run. There are certain elements that we must experience, only occasionally we experience a break from it, if we maintain enough effort.

"Nothing comes from nothing" is how a lady teacher addressed students in her classes. Success in education cannot be instantly measured with school marks.

As I write today, it is part of my understanding that events in our life always serve a purpose. A conclusion should be delivered through events to get a dialogue between a writer and a reader started. A reader does not necessarily have to agree fully with the conclusion, but he should be encouraged to compare events. This is what makes a reader.

Let me again continue with the events of my teenage life. Not every school holiday turned into a holiday. Young people have wishes to test their real goals in life. Satisfied wishes create a strong self confidence, as long as such achievements are based on strong personal efforts. My mother used to say: "A wish as soon as it is fulfilled, creates many more wishes."

I started part-time work to fulfill a first wish of an income during the school holidays. Dad offered me a variety of work in the factory. He wanted to see if I could follow in his footsteps. At this age, I could not consider anything else but to familiarize myself with the new working environment. I enjoyed my working holiday. The money was not much in those days, but the reward from such work put me in a position to fulfill modest wishes on my own terms. I soon realised that standing all day made me tired after a day's work thus school again became a welcome change after this work experience.

Biology was a subject which attracted my attention at school. Our teacher taught biology and mathematics. In biology, the teacher took our class from time to time out into the fields surrounding our town and to the nearby forest. Everybody loved such excursions because it was easier to comprehend our studies rather than just learning from a text book. One biology excursion, not far from school, the class received instructions to keep close together as we walked past two council street cleaners. Somebody out of our group called them a commonly known derogatory nickname "Stadtlaucher" (town leak).

The cleaners reacting by picking somebody out of the group who they thought had delivered this insult. They picked on me even though I had nothing to do with that insult. Our teacher joined in. When he heard what happened, I was declared the scapegoat and received a sound bashing in front of everybody. This was the end of this excursion. The whole class had to return to the school and the punishment continued with a mathematics test.

Rigorous conditions applied to these results, with the marks out of this test counting double.

By the next day, we had all cooled down. Everybody in the class actually knew who the real offender was and that I had copped the 'shits' for the wrong reason.

The next day when the teacher arrived, he turned straight towards me offering his extended hand and congratulating me for the best test result.

I had never excelled in mathematics, but this time I was the only one who gained 100% – far in front of the rest of the class. Our teacher must have received the correct message about the incident from the day before. I was assured the case was forgotten and the teacher declared: "Martin you will have credit for a bashing in the future." My relationship with this teacher continued undisrupted from then on.

My interest in biology also became obvious at home. With my own hands I built a complete dovecot under the roof of a shed. A small number of homing pigeons, which came from a friend, found a home in my dovecot. I spent hours with my pigeons, observing them, trying to understand more about their way of life. I could occasionally move my pigeons with a special box into another place to understand how they returned home without failure. After the pigeons were released out of their box away from home, they circulated the sky for a while until one of them indicated the direction home. Migrant birds have a sense to follow magnetic field lines of our earth to reach destinations.

Wind directions and light characteristics from our sun are taken equally in consideration. It is quite a complex sense of direction and pigeons have a similar sense.

I raised young pigeons at home as well. It was a great fascination for me, but it wasn't long until dad decided that the pigeons took up too much of my time and I should be concentrating on my school work. The dovecot had to be shut down and abandoned to my great disappointment.

My relationship with animals could now only continue with my cat, but she could never make up for my homing pigeons.

'Tour de France'

There was one more holiday that I shared with my parents. Dad developed contacts with a company in France, just on the outskirts of Paris. This company employed dad as a consultant. We combined a tour of Northern France in our Volkswagen with dad's work with the company. This trip allowed me to pick up some useful French language. At first, the French language was difficult even though I had learned it at school. The longer we stayed in France, the more I could communicate with people and thus gained an improved understanding of the language.

Mum and dad spoke French more fluently, because at home in Romania, French was the first foreign language.

During our tour we visited the towns of Reims and Rouen. The cathedrals in both towns were outstanding – very old and rich in cultural history. The busy harbour of Rouen indicated to us that the North Sea was not very far away.

On our tour we also followed waterways where ships appeared in the middle of typical landscapes with hedges around cornfields and weeping willows bordering stretches of roads. Most nights we spent in a tent until we reached Rouen. Caravans were rarely seen in those days.

The place we stayed overnight was more a camping place than a caravan park. Mosquitoes visited us in their thousands during the night. Mum said to just ignore this pest, but I could not sleep at all, spending all night fighting the mosquitoes. Next morning the outcome of mum's ' just ignore them discipline' became obvious. Mum's face was swollen up by mosquito bites and dad had sacrificed most of his night's sleep in a battle with the pest.

Our arrival in Rouen had to be postponed for a couple of days until mum's face was again presentable to the public. Our tour became more official in Rouen. A young lady student working with the company near Paris joined us to assist in language interpretation. Our destination was not, at first, Paris. Instead we were directed to the sea resort of Pont Au De Mer. We stopped at a small, beautiful, white hotel next to the beach.

Dad spent the next couple of days in the company near Paris, from where he returned each night. The accommodation in the hotel offered every possible luxury. Even the white graveled paths through the gardens were meticulous – always clean and perfectly level. For our two weeks here, our days on the beach started with a swim in shallow waters, which stretched along a fine light-brown stretch of sand. Fine summer weather attracted a large number of beachgoers.

Children played with a small rubber ball attached to a rubber band and a box on the ground. This set-up allowed a number of people to play the game and the ball remained securely attached to the rubber band and the box in the sand. People called this game 'jockary escoal'. I joined the children in the game – it really didn't matter whether I could speak enough French, children always find a way to communicate. It was here that I received my best French lessons.

When dad came back on the weekend, he brought along a set of 'jockary escoal' for us. The beauty of this ball game was that it only required a small area, one or more people can play the game and nobody has to run after the ball. The aim of this game was to get the ball on a very fast return and hit it in almost any direction.

When life is at its best, we savour the moment.

We had life lessons in French, we experienced French cuisine, beach life and, on top of everything, beautiful summer weather and could not ask for more.

Dad fulfilled his task at our host's place near Paris and we were ready to return home.

The year 1957 arrived on our calendar. Life in Ettlingen became easier as the war retreated further into the distance.

People started to think more positively about a future in Germany. As everything started small in our lives, these signs of a positive future were hardly visible. For lots of people, the recovery from war time did not happen in the way many had wished.

During these years a number of Germans packed up and tried their luck somewhere else. Mum's brother moved with his family to Brazil. Dad took a firm stand and decided to stay where we were.

Realistically, everything we do in life with consistency will lead to something.

My life focused mainly on school: fees and having to supply my own materials made my education very expensive for my parents at that time. Many could not afford to continue education on a 'higher' level, but my parents apparently could.

I still attended the boy scout movement in town, spent time practicing music – mostly outside home – and enjoyed athletics. There was not much free time left after these activities.

Holiday time arrived and dad had the idea to find some hard work for me so that I could build my strength. Some days I managed my back problem better than other days. In the north of our Black Forest, near Freudenstadt, was a place called Besenfeld where we enjoyed many excursions. The biggest farm in the place had a hotel next door called Oberwiesenhof where people from towns like Pforzheim could eat in comfort and experience a little bit of Black Forest country life. Here there was roast deer, roast wild pig, geese, milk, freshly-made butter, hand-picked forest berries, mushrooms out of the forest – all in all, whoever could pay for this was welcome. We were there one sunny, winter day when the heavy snow layers covered the Black Forest fir trees. I enjoyed my first skiing lessons on open fields outside the forest. Dad was a good skiing teacher because of his experiences in the Transylvanian mountains. During a snack in the hotel, Dad asked the farmer's son, who looked after the hotel, if his farm needed a helping hand for a few weeks over summer. Such a question had not often been raised by guests. The farmer's son responded to our question very quickly and we were invited to inspect his farm. The old farmer wanted me to start straight away, because his assistant just had left him. The farm was kept in a very good condition but it was too large to be managed by only one person. Farmer Muller agreed to see me again, when summer came in a few months time.

Our meeting took place in the farmhouse, which was the first part of a long building which included a hay storage floor. Work rooms, like the central milking station, were underneath this hay floor, then followed the cow sheds. The dung hill was located at the end of this long building.

Another lower building stood parallel on the opposite side with pig sties, storage facilities and an empty dwelling used for a farm assistant. The space between those buildings formed a yard that led uphill to the main road to Besenfeld.

The lounge in the farmhouse had everything covered with white linen to protect against the dust. Everything was cleanliness with added shine. What a perfectly uncomfortable environment to live in, I thought. Only important visitors received attention in this room, which was never used. Daily farm life was restricted to the kitchen and dining room. Farmer Muller promised to make a strong man out of me. We then returned home before nightfall.

It was winter and carnival time in Ettlingen. All the young people dressed up for the carnival which was a very much-anticipated event.

Groups of Indians and cowboys met throughout town and our boy scout groups also dressed in carnival costumes and sat around a fireplace at the carnival swapping stories and making plans. Everything was peaceful until hundreds of Indians and cowboys met in a field on the western outskirts of town. Some of the older youth were on horseback.

I watched as this crowd of opponents moved towards each other. I became frightened and moved back to town as quickly as I could.

This was supposed to be a harmless 'picture book' confrontation by the youth from Karlsruhe, but it soon turned ugly and lots of young carnival-goers were injured.

A real 'wild west' scene unfolded when a number of horse riders started to use live ammunition. The police were called in and a number of people were detained.

Nothing like this had ever happened before or ever happened again. Many burned their fingers with that incident.

It is anybody's guess where such aggression had come from. TV was not common during that time so that it wasn't the influence. A small number of youth, too old for such a carnival game, had started the aggression. Perhaps they thought it was part of their passage into adulthood. Years of war followed by years of stagnation had prepared the ground for an explosive demand for progress. Aggressive behaviour surfaced as a part of an individual expression.

Meanwhile, summer was closing in and my working holiday was approaching quickly. Before I left, we received a visit from cousin Fred's parents. The topics of school and education became a heated debate. Everybody claimed they were the better parent. It was during this argument that I first heard that I was adopted. I had no answer to such statement. I felt abandoned. To whom did I belong now? I never asked any questions, but became more reserved towards my step-parents. They must have realised this change and took quick action to make up for their neglect. A solicitor created a document where the ownership of me was cemented. I did not understand such a process.

Life continued, but my unease from this knowledge of my adoption surfaced from time to time. Seeing a picture of my biological parents could not change my attitude. I remained sad about the whole issue.

Work Experience

Summer holidays arrived. It was good for me to go away and think about other issues in my life. On a Saturday, Dad delivered me to the doorsteps of Muller's farm in Besenfeld. Mrs Muller showed me my bedroom in the farmhouse under the gable. The bed was fitted with a heavy thick cushion and a quilt filled with goose feathers from the farm. That was the only item of furniture in the room – a bed.

Holidays don't exist on a farm. Every day the duties were feeding the cows, the geese, the pigs and cleaning at exactly the same time early in the morning and late in the afternoon. The time in between was used to distribute the hay, deliver the milk and homemade butter to the hotel and to the town. I also had to collect chicken eggs, maintain the farm equipment and occasionally go to the farm's forest where logs for pulp paper had to be worked on. Only Sunday was the exception. Farmer Muller spent most Sundays in the forest on his tractor with a gun for hunting. Nobody else went with him.

I started work on the farm as soon as I arrived. I was given a pair of gumboots and started in the cow shed with Farmer Muller.

An elevated passage ran through the centre of the shed. To the left and right were feeding baskets in a row with the cows behind them.

The cows knew exactly their feeding time. The whole shed was filled with the mooing of the cows. As soon as they received molasses, hay and a mixture of grain in their baskets, they changed their sound to a calm, monotonous chewing. We then joined the cows through a downstairs connection. Farmer Muller told me to be cautious when approaching the cows because they did not know me. "Always move to the side of a cow, never from behind," he said. I just missed being kicked by a cow when I tried to put the milking tubes on the udders for the first time. A cow will let you know very quickly if you are doing the right thing by her. When a person pulls the udders gently to prepare the cow for the milking tubes, the cow knows who the person is. The cow makes her point very clear when she does not like the approach. The milk can will certainly be displaced if her kick misses the person. The size of the udders tells the expert which cow to milk first.

While the cows fed, the old wood dust on the ground was replaced with new dust. For the night-time only straw was added and this became one of my duties. As soon as the cow sheds were cleaned, Farmer Muller started the milking process. All milk cans were moved to the adjacent processing room and were emptied into a big shiny container. Mrs Muller looked after that side. She separated an exact quantity of the thick milk layer that formed on top of the container to make butter. A china can was filled with milk straight from the cow and this ended up on my breakfast table. Fresh milk from a cow might sound healthy, but I could not drink it. I secretly disposed of this milk in the wash basin next to the kitchen table – without the farmer's knowledge.

After tending the cows, the pigs were cleaned and fed close towards the evening. The pigs were the first in the morning to announce a new day, exactly at 5am, regardless of the weather. Pigs must have a built-in alarm clock. If we didn't arrive at five o'clock, they started their pig noises.

One particularly large pig had the incredible number of 15 young piglets. Only Farmer Muller or his wife could enter the box where the pig lay down on straw to allow the piglets to freely feed on her. Farmer Muller could pick up a piglet, have a look at it and return it to the mother under her watchful eyes. As soon as I attempted to get close, the sow started to get up on her legs, dropping all her babies on to the straw underneath her while making a repeated deep warning sound. Those piglets later became a delicacy on the hotel's menu.

I found pigs to be very alert creatures with a sense of curiosity. They reacted immediately to any changes with their typical pig noise.

In Muller's pigsties also lived a huge wild boar. When he was out in the yard, somebody had to control him. Farmer Muller showed me how this was done: "Hit the boar with your gumboots as hard as you can, only this way will he receive a message and respect you". Farmer Muller was right. I also managed to control the boar this way.

A few weeks later, this boar was slaughtered by Farmer Muller. I did not like this action at all. A needle between his front legs brought the boar down immediately. The boar must have known his fate. The pigs in the sheds responded to his calls. The moment the boar passed away, total silence took over in the sheds.

Blood was first taken of the boar to make a large quantity of sausages with the intestines. The boar lay on a board outside in the yard, boiling water over his body helped to clean the hair from the skin. After the body was opened with a knife, thus began many hours of carving. The boar weighed over 500 kilograms. Farmer Muller processed selected meats, sausages were cooked in a large kettle, some meat ended up in a smoking chamber, other meats went into a freezer. Everything of the boar was processed.

Most people have no idea the amount of work that goes into processing meat before it reaches the table. It is a necessity to slaughter, but it is also controversial. I found, with reservations, that it was useful to be present during the slaughtering process – at least to discover a new-found respect for life.

Every lunch time I was allowed to go to the hotel and choose from a number of pots on the stove. Roast deer became my favourite lunch. I had the best of food on that farm.

After a day's work I went to the farmhouse kitchen where I was served brown bread slices with butter, smoked ham and the can of fresh cow's milk, which I couldn't stand. Every night, the same was on my table.

The days on the farm were long. I woke at a quarter to five in the morning and finished my day by 8 o'clock at night. These long days made me so tired, I fell asleep as soon as I went to bed.

One of our hardest days of work was when we went to the farm forest on the tractor. Farmer Muller, already in his early seventies, worked the logs on the forest ground so hard that I could not keep up with him.

We had to pull out fallen fir trees on a chain with our tractor – a highly dangerous operation. One had to watch very carefully to ensure the tree was constantly moving and not building up tension on the chain behind the tractor. If the chain tension built up, the log could suddenly jerk towards the tractor. People had been killed on such occasions. I had to cut branches off with a hand saw, before the tree logs were pulled with the tractor on to a forest path. The logs were cut into two metre lengths with a long hand saw. The logs were loaded on a wagon and when that wagon was full, we returned to the farm. I found this work especially hard. There was already a pile of logs at the farmyard. Farmer Muller showed me how to strip the bark off the logs. He encouraged me to do this work in my spare time after a day's work. A sawhorse secured the log, while I worked the bark with a slightly curved knife blade which had a handle at both ends. I had to make sure that I cut the bark off and nothing else. I very quickly developed the required skills and experienced a sense of pride, when I looked at the growing pile of cleaned logs. I had high hopes that I would receive an extra bonus for the cleaned logs.

One Sunday afternoon I was spending my spare time log cleaning while Farmer Muller was hunting in his forest. A lady with her two daughters came past me to have a look at the farm. I said hello but they preferred to ignore me. I was not sure whether they came from a foreign country so I addressed them cautiously in English and then French. The ladies must have become upset about the way I welcomed them.

Are there people out in the world, who limit their horizon towards other people? I thought about this incident later. The ladies must have become confused by a farm worker, who could address them in English and then in French, after they didn't respond in German. It could have been the start of an interesting conversation – if they had said something. All people are different and so is their understanding.

One night on the farm, a noise from the cow shed woke me up. A few moments later Farmer Muller arrived at my bedroom door. "Martin, my cow is in labour. She can't make it, we need to help," he said. We rushed down to the shed. Farmer Muller handed me some ropes to secure them around a post while he immobilised the cow with the loose ends of the rope. The back legs of the cow were bound together to keep the hoofs under control. The farmer must have known, what he was doing. Just as the calf's front legs emerged, he tied them together with another rope, which was attached to another post for traction.

The operation to pull the calf out began. Unfortunately the calf did not survive. The farmer became very upset and sent me back to my bedroom.

Next morning I was shocked to see the calf in the dung hill.

Life continued on the farm: we had to leave behind what we could not control.

The Mullers also taught me how to pluck the farm geese. The plucking was done by Mrs Muller. She sat down on a chair in a separate room with one door accessing the geese pen. The geese were highly alert – they knew from previous times that they had to give something. Mrs Muller knew her role. The question was, who would catch one goose at the time and bring it to her. I tried my luck with the advice given to me. Muller's geese were very well fed. To carry a goose, I had to grab its neck close to its head with a firm grip of my left hand. My right hand went quickly around the goose's body in front of its legs, then I pulled the whole goose up from the ground and tucked it under my right arm. When I gave the goose to Mrs Muller, she remained on her chair and took the body of the goose between her legs, reminding me to keep the head away from her. I lost my grip on the neck of one goose during this exercise. Its beak reached Mrs Muller's wrist with lightning speed and she suffered a badly bruised arm. She rose from her chair, shouting: "You sleepy head!" I had to assure her I would not make the same mistake again. She carried on, holding the body of the goose firmly between her legs, one arm controlling the goose, the other went under each wing plucking the fine feathers. This job turned out not to be an easy one. The feathers were destined for quilts in the hotel, where guests paid good money for the 'illusion' of enjoying a weekend of farm life.

My illusion came to a sudden end, when dad arrived to pick me up after six weeks. We all met in the living room, where everything was still covered with white sheets.

Farmer Muller expressed his satisfaction with my work efforts, which was nice to hear at least at the end of my six weeks. I had already a number of plans on how to spend my pay. In particular, I wanted to buy a good wristwatch. The pay came on the scene very quickly. Farmer Muller handed me one single bank note of 100DM. I hesitated to take the single bank note and looked confused at Farmer Muller and dad. I could not hide my disappointment with this small amount of remuneration. I had worked 14 hours a day, seven days a week during my stay on the farm. The farmer's response was: "You ate in the hotel kitchen, slept in our house and the other meals were also free." Tears of disappointment appeared in my eyes. Dad joined the farmer in the next room, leaving me alone for a while. Dad had nothing to say when he returned.

I started to think, what was the purpose of this farm stay? No wonder Farmer Muller remained alone with all the work. I learned to swallow here a bitter pill.

The farmer wanted to impress dad showing him his wine cellar. Steps led deep under the house to the cellar. Farmer Muller returned with a bottle in his hand. It was totally covered in mould. He said: "This is a red wine out of the last century. Hotel guests pay 1000DM for one bottle, if you want one, you can buy one."

Dad thanked him for such generous offer and then we left. On the way home, Dad offered to contribute to my efforts so that I could at least fulfill my dream of owning a wristwatch.

What a lesson I learned now! Going back to school again was like going back into another world. I became more determined from this day on with my own goals.

Dad had to handle a lot of stress in his company position. As a result he had become less and less patient with me and mum. A position a person holds doesn't always fit a person. We do a lot of things in life that we are not qualified for. Conflict can build up in us and this can affect other people. Once this happens, it can make life for all involved uneasy. A young person like me looked at life from a different angle.

We have to meet on the same level to understand each other or else the gap in an understanding widens.

I remember two incidents. One happened to a good friend, the other to me. The friend was playing with an airgun in his backyard upsetting the neighbour. Swear words were exchanged across the fence until the police were called. My friend went back into his home and tried to hide. Soon after the police turned up demanding to speak to his father. The police relayed their version of the incident, whereas the father of my friend played down the whole situation stating: "There is no gun and nobody is shooting here." The neighbour's allegations lost ground and the case became settled in a friendly way.

Now, to my incident, which happened around the same time. Mum did her shopping in a milk store close to home, near the railway station. She waited in a queue while I mucked around in the park next to the railway station.

I mumbled something to myself – what I really can't remember. A town street sweeper thought he heard something he didn't like and started to chase me. In my confusion, I did the wrong thing and rushed across the road to the shop where mum was. I did not look for traffic because I was so frightened. I took refuge in the shop with mum. The man followed on my heels raising a 'stink' in front of mum. Mum promised to look into it and to teach me a lesson at the same time. When mum told dad, he lost his cool and

I received a flogging with the leather belt which was always ready on the hook behind the kitchen door.

Two incidents, two completely different outcomes. My outcome did not help to improve an understanding with my dad. I retreated in silence.

Once I became the observer of a rare incident within our family. Dad always requested to have lunch served at the same time – even though he was far more flexible, when it came to him being on time. He always offered the excuse that his responsibilities at the company sometimes prevented him from being on time. Mum used to wait patiently until dad arrived.

One day she made pancakes for lunch and dad turned up one hour late without notifying her. The pancakes had turned sticky, hurting her pride. Mum lost her temper and the pancakes ended up flat and nicely in the middle of dad's face with the words: "Here you have got your lunch on time." The 'storm' cleared the air on the spot.

With my new-found determination I decided to finish gymnasium after class six. A final celebration used to take place at that level with the class and all the teachers. We met in the function room of a local restaurant on a Saturday night. It was a successful celebration in a very friendly atmosphere.

Apprentice years

An uncle convinced me over a period of time to start an apprenticeship as a toolmaker. His sense for accuracy was the trigger for my decision. Dad could not agree on it and tried in vain to convince me to follow in his footsteps and become a paper engineer. A company near our gymnasium was testing a number of applicants for a toolmaking apprenticeship. Only a few were selected and I was proud to be one of them.

I had now reached a turning point. I was out of school and new rules applied. I had to be ready for work at 7am every day, including Saturday. I had to be clean and tidy. A modern, progressive company demanded this image. An apprentice master was in charge of the training. He demanded respect and discipline. The new apprentices were allocated to a place on a workbench. Everybody received a number of hand tools, which were stored in drawers under the workbench. It was our responsibility to maintain these tools. The apprentice-master stood between two work benches and showed us how to use the measuring instruments. He demonstrated the vernier measuring device and how its smooth movement could be used for a correct measurement. Every apprentice moved his vernier as shown. During this task, I dropped my vernier on the timber lattice floor in front of me. This sound of a dropped vernier alarmed the master. He stood straight in front of me, slapped my face and said: "You will never drop a vernier again!" And indeed I never did.

An apprenticeship in those days was a privilege in further education. The company expected the apprentices to do their utmost to succeed in their training after the probation period. Our first test was to file an exact shape. This exercise lasted over a week and everybody's hands were blistered as a result. Four weeks later, the blisters were forgotten and we had got used to spending all day on our feet. The physical training had stopped and we now learned how to operate various machine tools. Technical drawings introduced us to the language of technology. Many detailed parts, manufactured to precise specifications, made a technical solution only, if everything was done correctly.

Lessons once a week within the factory supported our learning process. Our own drawings and handwritten reports had to be presented on that day. A vocational school also contributed one day a week to our training. This apprenticeship gave me much pleasure. The teachers, who were recruited from the real world, differed from the gymnasium's teachers. Their close co-operation with our work place ensured our progress.

The uncle, who had advised to do this apprenticeship, also told me that he had undertaken studies with an engineering institution. These studies attracted my interest so I took up these courses from the beginning of my apprenticeship.

The company's managing director approached me one day as I was struggling with an automated labeling machine. "The company needs somebody in our design department. Are you interested?" I did not hesitate one moment.

The company, the oldest aircraft manufacturer in the country, only promoted people from within their own staff. The boss in the engineering section also came from a toolmaking background. Graduate engineers worked under his supervision. Only the best became the boss. In those days it was necessary to keep abreast of the ever-changing technology.

I still was under the supervision of the apprentice master when I started my work on a drawing board. To work for two bosses was a challenge for me. The boss in the engineering department had reservations about my appointment. Everyone's work was scrutinized by everybody in the department from time to time, because it is a known fact that an individual is the last one to see their own mistakes.

One day I was at the boss' drawing board and while looking at his work found something, that didn't look right. I asked him: "How is that tool holder going in and out in the machine turret?" The boss looked at his drawing, then at me. But he reacted differently from what I had expected. First he said to the draftsman next to him: "Why didn't you see this and tell me?"

Then he said to me: "Go back to your board, stay there and don't rub your nose into other people's business!" I did as I was told but from then on personal politics started to set in. As an apprentice I had to avoid any conflict of interest. Our managing director must have heard, what was happening and solved the problem by telling me: "Martin you work on projects that I give you. When they are finished and I have approved them, go into the toolroom and make them."

Fair enough, I thought, this stops unnecessary controversy. I learnt a lesson to keep my nose out of other people's business, look after my own area and only have an opinion when asked for one.

Life in a factory is not much different from life in any other workplace – you have your ups and downs. An incident with a fellow apprentice highlighted the outstanding character of our managing director. A transistor radio had disappeared out of a locked cupboard in the change room. One night, when everybody was about to leave, I became aware of the strange behaviour of a fellow apprentice. I came straight to the point and said: "Have you got something to do with this radio?" He was very embarrassed and a lengthy conversation followed between us. I knew his background. His mother struggled to bring up four children. He was the oldest one and lucky to have an apprenticeship. His father went missing during the war. The radio was something he couldn't afford as an apprentice wage was just 40DM a month.

He revealed that he did have the radio so I urged him to confess to the managing director before the police started investigations the next day. My fellow apprentice did co-operate and visited the managing director at his home.

The outcome was unconventional and uncomplicated: the police were kept out, the radio was returned, silence became the order and our mate continued his apprenticeship. A penalty was imposed for him to pay half of his wages into a nominated account for the next six months. A written agreement was also signed. And that was that.

Twenty years later, when I went to Germany on a business trip from Brazil, I was in Ettlingen to visit my parents. As I walked through town, a flash Mercedes stopped next to me and the driver called out my name. I did not recognise him. "Don't you recognise your fellow apprentice from 20 years ago?" said the driver. I accepted his invitation to give me a lift to my parents' house. He told me he was the managing director of a highly-recognised technical development company. He had a wife and children and was supporting his mother. He rushed to open the car door for me and thanked me for my support 20 years ago. What a fantastic outcome!

During my apprenticeship years, life was not just work. I continued my hobbies of sports and music, but less time was available for my boy scout activities.

The Alps

I also had holidays during my apprenticeship, but not as long as school holidays. On one holiday it was decided to pull the bicycle out again. A friend suggested a tour through the Alps, I joined in and off we went. My friend treated this event like a race from the start and I had problems keeping up with him. Our bicycles were loaded with a tent, clothes, cooking gear with dishes and food. In other words, our legs had plenty to push along. The weather decided not to favour us and it rained for the whole 10 days of this tour through Bregenz, Liechtenstein, Innsbruck and Munich. We averaged 150km every day. The whole tour turned out to be a non-stop race. My friend proved his fitness, but I hated this type of holiday. In Innsbruck we tried hard to find time to relax – the purpose of a holiday. Instead we found ourselves, together with other holidaymakers, waiting for the rain to stop. Our interest in sightseeing became significantly reduced, when everything got wet – ourselves and our gear. Nothing stopped us from heading home. What a holiday, I said to myself, a race to try and leave the rain behind. Back at home, Murphy's law applied, it was brilliant sunshine!

On a positive note, we started and finished the tour together. Afterwards, however, we lost contact with one another.

The Alps showed me their sunny side on another occasion. My mum and dad took me to Tyrol in early spring of the following year. Near Bolzano we entered the small valley of Schnalls Tal. The road stopped at the base of the mountains. All the houses were in the lower part of this valley. Surrounded only by a few islands of fir-tree forest, a farmhouse with an inn waited for guests like us. I did not have to work here. I just had to enjoy myself. The inn was built in typical local style with massive timber logs, an elevated veranda in the front and a steep gable roofed over the entire building. Flower baskets on the veranda rail were yet to bloom. Snow fields still covered the upper mountain slopes.

We were in the Oetztaler Alps and right in front of us, to the north, was the mighty peak of the Weisskugel rising to a height of 3800 metres. The inn was built on an elevated bank near the river and was out of the way of possible avalanches.

During the daytime, the sun warmed up this mountain air quite comfortably. At night the temperature dropped below freezing point. Huge feather quilts on our beds ensured a good night's sleep; memories of Besenfeld in the Black Forest came rushing back to me.

Here in the narrow upper part of the valley daylight came through the mountains later and left earlier than at home, making a day here shorter.

The whole farmer's family, old and young, went about their farm business during the day, while we took the opportunity to discover the area on foot. The sun shone every day out of a crystal clear sky. Ice crystals on the snow surface reflected the light very intensively so sunglasses were a must. Most of the time we walked, where snow had melted away. Fresh mountain air gave us the feeling that our lungs were filled to the brim. We were the only guests at the inn and our days passed peacefully.

One day of our stay we joined the locals on the bus to Merano. To get to the bus stop, we had to walk down a distance through the valley on a rocky road.

The scene around us changed quickly – the islands of forest grew larger. Our road was so narrow that oncoming traffic had to stop to allow the other car to get past. Mum became very sick during this bus tour and frightened, when she saw through the bus window just how close our bus came to the edge of the road. For the few locals this must have been just another bus trip to Merano.

We could not believe the changes in the landscape, when we just a short time later arrived in Merano. Palm trees welcomed us midst a colourful market place crowded with people. The temperature here allowed us to put away all our warm clothes and adjust ourselves to summer.

The same bus returned us late on the same day to our high valley. We had to walk to the inn in darkness.

The area was so interesting. The inn was in Austria, whereas Merano lay in Italy. People spoke the language of their country, but at the same time they communicate with each other using the dialect of Tyrol.

One morning I looked around the farm building. A young lady called me into the cow shed and asked: "Have you ever milked a cow?" I told her about my experience in the Black Forest insisting that I should show her how it was done. I gave it a try, pulling the udders gently without success. Not a drop of milk reached the clean bucket underneath. Then the lady demonstrated how she did it and, in fact, milk started to flow. She smiled at me – who knows what she was thinking.

I returned a bit confused to the inn. Our holiday in this idyllic corner of our world drew to its end. A good holiday experience positively nourished our daily lives for some time.

Berlin

In August 1960 I also had some holidays up my sleeve and decided to visit Berlin with a friend for a week. Our visit to the Eastern part of Berlin opened our eyes as to how the Communist East really looked.

The wall to keep all of its people in the 'eastern paradise' was built shortly after.

To get to Berlin, my friend and I decided to give hitch-hiking a try. With one exception, everything worked in our favour. In this instance, a driver pulled over to pick us up like any other time. The difference with this lift however became clear very quickly after the driver joined the traffic on the autobahn.

The weather showed its 'miserable face' on this day and it was cold and wet. We were keen to get off the road in this weather. Once we were in, the driver put his foot down on the accelerator overtaking all the other cars. We made an effort to discourage our driver from driving dangerously.

Berlin Wall built 1961

Poor knowledge of our language, a mess in the car and the driver's behaviour also made us suspicious. His jacket slipped to one side of his shoulder indicating that he carried something heavy in his pocket. He must have understood when I warned him: "If something silly happens, we all will end up on the other side of the road". In addition we showed him the contents of our backpacks so he knew there was nothing to gain from us. On the next exit we convinced him to stop and let us out. The moment we got out of the car, we rolled down the slope on the side of the road to get out of his sight. Only then we realised that the car had no number plates. We must have had a lucky escape. No other incident occurred during the rest of this trip. This part of the autobahn to Berlin led through East Germany and there were signs everywhere saying: "Stopping is illegal, east border control will respond immediately!"

This was meant to stop people-trafficking.

Berlin welcomed us with sunshine. The West of this city displayed normal activities with its traffic, shops busy with people and cafes along the pavements inviting everyone for a rest. Some parts of the city still showed with the 'Hollow Dent' – the destruction from World War Two.

Berlin, rebuilt centre

Many museums exhibited cultures from around the world. Museum Dahlem has Rembrandt's Man with the Golden Helmet and artifacts of Queen Nephrite from ancient Egypt. The exhibits of ancient Egypt were especially interesting. All in all, West Berlin could offer something for everybody. Its people are famous for displaying a sense of humour that is typical of the 'Berlin Snout'. On a sunny weekend we joined these Berliners at Wan See Lake. The shores of this lake were packed with people enjoying picnics, swimming, playing games, music and conversations. They made the best out of their situation even though West Berlin was still an occupied zone of Western Allies in the middle of a communist eastern region under the watchful eye of Russia.

During our visit we also watched a Formula 1 car race on the 'Avus'. The spectators watched from the centre of the track as the cars roared at full speed into a 180 degree curve that was sloped at 90 degrees. During that race, one of the drivers came over the top of this curve and he landed in the middle of a busy road. He did not survive this 'flight'.

When I talk about a pulsing city in West Berlin, East Berlin was a completely different world. We received permission to visit East Berlin during the daylight hours of one day only. The train to East Berlin was almost empty. A large number of military personnel entered the train at the border crossing. The whole trip took only a few minutes. The station at Alexander Place was without people and visible activities.

On the wide roads of Alexander Place there were few people and even fewer vehicles. It looked like a ghost town. Massive building blocks lined both sides of these roads without any sign of life. Further east, the roads and houses narrowed. Ugly brick house walls rose from the ground, people near a store went along their business in slow motion with sorry faces. Nobody wanted to talk to us, everybody seemed to be scared of something. The store, which was exclusively for Western customers, had near-empty shelves. The prices were not attractive because we were asked to pay in our own currency the same amount shown in theirs. We experienced the same disappointment at a bookshop where we had hoped for some bargains. We tried to visit a museum, but it was closed. A huge sign on the building informed us: "Museum closed, exhibits stolen by the West". We cut short our visit to East Berlin and turned our backs on this sad environment.

What a difference political systems can make to the same people of a city like Berlin. This profound experience enabled me to later write successfully on the subject of Democracy versus Communism. The president of the Federal Republic of Germany, Theodor Heuss, awarded me a special book prize for this essay.

When we returned to West Berlin, we only had time to take in a couple more sights, before we had to return home.

My intention in writing is not to challenge any tourist guide. Rather, I restrict myself to events, objects and people, how I came across them and how they influenced my life, no matter how significant or insignificant they might appear at a first glance.

There is a saying: "Everything starts off small." It is the small things in our lives that matter, they are with us all the time. If big things happen, they may come at any time. It is like climbing a ladder – one step at a time can bring us to the top, a big step could cause us to fall off.

An example of small steps is found in Berlin's City Hall of Schoeneberg. In this building was the Freedom Bell which rang every day at noon with a piercing, deep sound that could be heard over the entire city – right into its eastern part. Some millions of signatures from American citizens were deposited here as a warranty to keep this city free. President Kennedy, as well as President Clinton, reassured the status of Berlin through their visit by confessing: "Ich bin ein Berliner" (I am a Berliner). The political destiny of Berlin after World War Two was connected largely to good relations with America. Only in 1989 did Russia's Gorbachow manage to steal this international political show by helping to reunite the two Germanys, including Berlin. Gorbachow had a view for the future: "Russia wants to deal with Europe, stability can only be achieved with a united Germany".

Gorbachow gave history a chance not to repeat itself. In this process, Berlin emerged to a significant metropolis, not only within Germany, but within the whole of Europe. The Berliners have since successfully built on this foundation with their unshakable attitude. I experienced Berlin at an early stage when nobody could predict what the city's future held. For me, Berlin was certainly worth the journey back then.

Back at home, my teacher at Vocational School urged me to participate in a writer's competition. The title was: "Democracy-Communism in today's world and the future". I could not miss this opportunity. I tackled the subject by focusing on key points and delivering answers to key questions. Neighbourhood systems will experience changes through positive and negative influences; this is one of nature's mechanisms to drive our existence.

The Vocational School handed my work to the Ministry of Culture. A few months later my teacher told me: "Your work won first price and you will receive a book with a personal comment from our President Theodor Heuss". My achievement was publicised in the local newspaper.

In this writer's competition I was considered the 'outsider', because all the other students came from 'higher levels'. I felt quite good about my success.

Mum and dad did their best to ignore my writing skills. They probably still had hopes of making a chemistry engineer out of me.

My work place responded to this achievement by asking me to write about our company. When I did, the company owner was not very impressed. In my view, the owner did not understand that writing to serve a purpose is not independent thought.

Independence requires freedom of expression.

Despite not scoring significant points with this appointment, I did learn a lesson: pleasing everybody is an impossible task!

Success in my life gave me some self-esteem. I was rather shy and a bit clumsy when it came to dealing with the 'fairer sex'. Convention tells us that the best way to get closer to a woman and impress her with a conversation is to dance with her. At previous school events, everybody danced to match the rhythm of the music.

Dance School

Dancing is an art that has to be learned. Mum and dad went to the expense of booking me into a noble dance course in the nearby city of Karlsruhe. The lady teacher was a champion dancer within Germany. Our Thursday night classes started with the basic dance routines. Male students on one side of the dance floor, females on the other side. The men step forward, one by one, select a female partner, bow in front of her, offer her their right arm and then step aside together and wait for further instructions. Men had to be dressed in a black suit with a bowtie, women in a long gown of their choice.

Step by step instructions followed: "Put your open right hand gently on the back of your partner, stretch the left hand horizontal to hold the other hand, one step forward, always upright, two smaller steps sidewise, half a turn together, watch other couples, do not look down at your feet, look at your partner. As soon as the dancing stops, stay with your partner and start a conversation, that can include other couples".

At the end of evening lessons, men were asked to accompany their partners on their way home. Our teacher ended the evening by performing a dance to demonstrate her own skills and what we could achieve.

I was the youngest student in this course and thus my conversations were not as interesting as the other older 'men of the world'. Most students were academics. When I was asked: "What are you doing for work?" and I answered "I am an apprentice toolmaker", dead silence confronted me. I tried to ignore this silence.

There were occasions when everybody was asked to turn up in casual clothes, mainly for modern dances like rock 'n' roll.

I enjoyed these dancing lessons and vastly improved my dancing skills.

After six months, the end of this course drew closer and a farewell party was organised. During these dancing lessons most students found a partner for this event, except for a small group to which I belonged. Finally a partner was chosen for everybody to take to the farewell party.

Male students were told to bring a bunch of flowers and dress in a black tailcoat suit with a silver bowtie. We were to pick up our dance partner from her home, give her the flowers, put on a brave face with a big smile and accompany our partner to the farewell party.

I did not like this formality. I could not imagine myself dealing with so much bullshit.

So I attended the school ball in my home town instead and the atmosphere there was just great. Everybody came dressed in clothes of his own choosing. This gave the party a colourful image and young people mixed freely.

Food, non alcoholic drinks, music, dancing, group plays and an occasional speech all made the party very enjoyable for everybody.

I danced most of that evening with a young schoolgirl – she must have liked our dancing. Then my pretty dancing partner told me she had to leave to catch the train home to Neurot, a place further up in our valley. She had no objection to me escorting her to the railway station. Before her train was due, I insisted: "Please tell me your name and we'll meet up again". A glance and a handshake sealed the deal.

Not long after that school party, slides from New Zealand were shown in the community hall of the local church. I told my parents about this event and they were interested to go with me. The community hall was packed with visitors. Just before we took our seats, Renate, the girl from Neurot, came past us with her mother. I introduced the two parties to one another and everybody was delighted. The slide show was an outstanding success. A screen reflected scenes of mountains, green pastures, rugged coastlines and volcanic activities. This far-away world seemed to everyone to be an image of paradise – far out of reach for ordinary people.

When the slide show was over, I approached Renate and her mother offering to escort them to the railway station and they accepted.

I was on track to having my first girlfriend. Even mum and dad were delighted. "Martin, you show very good taste," they said. I was on top of the world! 'Who flies high, can fall from great heights' – but concerns like this could not bother me at that time, first love was in the air. My days could not pass fast enough for me to contact Renate again. I didn't use the phone very often, because her mum usually picked up the call first. The last thing I wanted was to appear obtrusive. This caution paid off and I was asked to come to their place and share a cup of tea with them next Sunday. I caught the train to their fantastic mansion. The doorbell was answered by Renate's grandmother.

I introduced myself and was escorted to the back of the house.

Moments later Renate rushed towards me and showed me the way to a bay-window, which had a view of their garden. I presented Renate with a flower from our garden. The house reflected a solid tradition.

The 'cup of tea' was a friendly meeting. The matron of the house must have held the principle that 'everything needs its time, never rush things'. Our cup of tea was allowed to last only for 20 minutes – my visiting time ran like sand in an hourglass. Renate then accompanied me to the door. My visit was over. Is brevity the soul of wit?

During this time I kept up my musical efforts. At boy scout meetings we learned classical guitar music. I won the co-operation of two of my best friends to perform a guitar serenade at Renate's house for her birthday.

We started playing in the garden and then were welcomed inside to join the extended family around a big round table. We received a warm welcome. Everybody seemed to like our way of saying 'happy birthday'. When it was asked, who was Renate's admirer, her mother said: "Mister Martin, you should build on your voice". Our serenade was a success and we were invited to sit at the table.

The atmosphere around the table could be called very conservative. Everybody was dressed in formal clothes, candles on the table reflected the lights from the chandelier.

Wine was served in crystal glasses, food waited on exquisite plates, questions circulated and an animated conversation took place. Renate's mother entertained her guests with the comment: "Mister Martin, you will live in a far-away country one day". What a prediction! Why did she say this?

Was she reading my mind into the future or testing something?

No matter what, she was right. Some 22 years later I was going to live in Australia. It is as far away as a place could be. I want to mention that in 1944 during the war, my stepmother made me a toy kangaroo for Christmas. I have never lost this toy during my eventful life. I firmly believe that 'everything in life is accidental'.

Our serenade evening came to its end before dusk, so Renate's mother did not have to worry how we would get home. As young as we were, and possibly also a bit naïve, we enjoyed our serenade evening.

My next meeting with Renate was at the opening of a new sports facility in my home town of Ettlingen. The facility was built at a sports club just on the outskirts of town under the initiative of the club's trainer Mr Kary. All the work was done on a voluntary basis by members of the TSV-Ettlingen – an incredible effort and a huge success.

Waiting for action and funds from other organisations was not an option and most certainly the club would not have got off the ground in those days without the years of personal sacrifices by these volunteers. At last the time had arrived for opening celebrations. For this occasion I asked Renate's mother for permission to take Renate to the celebrations.

A friend of mine helped out by driving me to Renate's home to pick her up. At that time I had a driver's licence but could not afford a car of my own. An apprenticeship in the late 1950s only paid a mere 40DM per month.

The celebrations in our new sports complex went well and featured a program of music, dancing, jokes, plays, food and drinks. Renate had to be back home at an appointed time and we delivered her home on time.

Slowly I realised that Renate depended very much on her mother's advice. There is, generally speaking, nothing wrong with that, but it did lead to a later disappointment.

Renate invited me to an event at a five-star hotel in Herrenalb. As I had no transport of my own, a couple of other party-goers were organised to pick me up. I didn't know them at all. The first introductions were difficult, and there was just enough room in their car to squeeze me in. During this short trip, not even one word was exchanged, which I thought very strange. At the hotel entrance, a 'pompously' dressed lady welcomed everybody individually with a handshake and everyone, except me, gave her flowers. I felt bad about this and could only try to hide my embarrassment. When we entered the saloon, I could not help but draw parallels to the dance lessons in Karlsruhe. The whole evening remained stiff and formal. I could not understand why Renate did not introduce me to the other guests, so I introduced myself. She only paid attention to other guests. I was left with the daughter of my former maths teacher from the gymnasium. The end of this strange meeting could not have come early enough for me.

Was this the answer to my informal invitation to the inauguration of our sports complex? I took this as a lesson that not everybody was as independent in his life as I was.

A cooling-off period followed and I made no further effort to see Renate anymore. My cousin Constance had nothing better to do but to tell me on my birthday that she saw Renate dancing very intimately with a university-student in Karlsruhe.

I decided, once and for all, to gain clarification of this situation. The same night I rode my bicycle the short distance to Renate's house. As I arrived at her house I could see Renate in the living room with another man. Renate had made her choice. This was the end of our relationship.

Black Forest

In the middle of the Black Forest lies a small town called Hornberg. The town is in the neighbourhood of Triberg, a watch manufacturing centre, where the cuckoo clock originates from.

My parents and I enjoyed a trip to this area. This is where the Black Forest got its name – tall black fir trees densely covered the slopes of the mountains. This forest had to give way to buildings mainly along the course of a river. Most of the buildings are the very old style of farmhouse typical of the Black Forest. The house is usually cut into the slope of a hill, its basement is constructed of sandstone blocks and the upper part of the house of a solid timber beam construction. A veranda is attached to the upper part of the house which is similar to houses in the Alpine areas of Switzerland, Austria, Italy and France. Colourful tubs of flowers give these houses a very nice look during summer.

It is the roof that makes the Black Forest house special as it reaches almost to the ground along the sides of the house. The old houses are covered with a shingle-roof of fumed timber – some roofs are covered with straw. As the house is cut out of a hill, the higher part of this hill is used for direct access into the top of the building to store hay for the winter. Underneath are the family rooms taking up two storeys, while the ground level holds the animal shelter. The dung hill is on the side of the house and dried timber-logs are stacked in front of the house. Everything in a Black Forest house lives close together – better to withstand the harsh winters.

A timber runner-sledge can occasionally be seen on the side of a house. Inside is mainly fitted with a fireplace and a tiled stove. A farming family traditionally dresses up on special days in their national costumes: mainly black clothes. The farmer wears a jacket with colourful front embroidery, his hat is also black with a wide rounded rim. The wife wears either a distinctly folded scarf or the legendary black hat, which has five fire-red fluffy balls on its rim. Her white blouse is taken up on the upper sleeves.

Our trip to Hornberg was, because dad wanted to visit a small factory, which had something to do with paper production. The family we were going to see was very nice. They had a daughter of my age and she invited me for a swim in their pool near the river. The pool water was freezing. Even though it was summer, only a few hours of sun reached this narrow valley between mountains every day – not enough time to warm up a river from where the pool drew its water. During a swim, I battered the pool water with all my force to shake off this cold. Tough people live here, I thought. A cup of hot tea restored my senses. Still today I hate cold water. Is that because of this experience in the Black Forest? Only later in Finland did I learn to adjust to cold water. They visit a sauna first before exposing themselves to the cold.

Our trip to Hornberg ended with our Black Forest hosts saying: "Please come and see us again soon".

I did return later to Hornberg by train on a Sunday morning. I brought my guitar as I wanted to bring my music to the Black Forest. From the railway station I announced my arrival by phone. Luck was on my side as the master of the house answered my call.

We planned how I would begin my guitar serenade. At first we thought I could start outside by scaling a ladder to the windows. But it was too much to ask for – climbing a ladder, hanging on to it, playing the guitar and singing! We decided that I should go to the entrance of the house and start playing. The surprise worked and after I began playing from behind the entrance door, I was asked to come in. Bay windows in the lounge surrounded a table with corner benches. The family sat on one side and I performed my serenade on the other side. I played for about an hour and received a friendly response. I could not stay much longer as I had to catch the train back home.

It should be pointed out that in those days everybody had to create their own entertainment to fill in their spare time. Television had not yet been introduced and, when it was, only a few could afford a couple of hours of daily broadcasting in black and white. The cinema was a popular entertainment with a variety of movies in black and white or colour. We all had to be active, if we wanted something.

In those days money couldn't take you as far as in 2007. But it was a good time for young people like us to grow up.

Meanwhile, my parents still wanted me to be a chemistry engineer. One day I found a magazine on my desk with an article about the shortage of chemistry engineers. The headline said: "Do you want to become a chemistry engineer?" In my young enthusiasm, I was quick to get a pen and attach to the front page a note saying 'no thank you!'

Well, a storm was unleashed when dad got hold of this magazine. If there was any respect left for me, it disappeared now once for all. I refused to be pushed into this career. I believed I had the right to make my own decisions. A war without words had started, but I was determined.

Even the best of intentions lead into a controversy if they are not addressed properly. This was my parents' fate with their son not responding to their wishes.

I had only one thing on my mind from now on – to finish my apprenticeship as soon as possible and start my own life.

The duration of my apprenticeship was reduced because of my hard efforts. Examination time arrived with one week of written tests and two hard days of practical tests in a local associated company.

The practical side with its high precision test pieces was much more demanding than the written tests. In the end I achieved excellent results in both disciplines and this boosted my confidence. The National Apprentice Board organised a tour of recognition for one week in Munich. On that occasion I attended a performance in a special opera house and the nearby German Museum of Technology, which was a great experience. The museum featured complete technology samples showing all stages of development. It was fascinating. The size of the museum and its abundance of information made the visit an unforgettable experience. Five-star hotel accommodation only added to the experience.

Black Forest tour

In March 1962, four members of our boy scout group had the idea of a walking tour through the Black Forest. We were inspired by President

Kennedy of America who said: "Every fit young man must be able to walk 70km with a backpack of 20kg within 24 hours". We were anxious to find out if we met this fitness test.

The Black Forest starts with its hills just outside our hometown of Ettlingen with a valley leading to its interior. At the end of the valley we had to climb the first heights of the Black Forest, and once we reached Dobel our walking tour continued at this height until we arrived in Freudenstadt, further south.

The weather was as one could only expect: a mixed bag of cold, sunny, rainy and – not to forget – windy. We all agreed that we would tackle the 70km walk one day towards the end of our excursion.

On the way we visited Besenfeld, the place, where I had worked on the farm six years earlier. The Hotel Oberwiesenhof was still there waiting for its customers. Nothing much had changed from the outside. The farm buildings were unchanged. We could not see anybody on the farm and so asked at the hotel if Mr and Mrs Muller still lived on the farm across the road. "Yes they do," came the reply. At the farm, the elderly couple gave us a warm welcome. They still remembered me.

The years had changed their way of life. Farmer Muller did not perform the hard work anymore. Our visit turned out to be a very short one because farmers aren't usually ready for surprise visits. We offered them a song before we left. Mrs Muller welcomed the offer saying: "Boys show me what the musical part of your heads can produce".

The northern highlands of the Black Forest were widely covered with blankets of snow. Most of the snow on the ground came from the fir tree branches that reflected a dark green-black image, which gave these forests their name.

Our next destination, Freudenstadt, lived up to its name of a 'city of joy'. This small town was completely rebuilt – no sign was left of the total destruction from World War Two.

We headed south through the ancient monastery of Alpirsbach following the upper Kinzig valley. Here the river Kinzig cuts its way through steep mountain slopes leaving little space. This rocky creek can become a rapid torrent that claims the whole valley, when the snow melts.

We left Kinzig valley from Schiltach and headed towards Lauterbach, a rural hamlet, which sits high up in the Black Forest. A few farm buildings in typical Black Forest style were spread some distance from one another.

Around these houses the forest had given way to open green meadows to allow cattle to roam during summer. We took a path from these remote Black Forest heights down to Gutach valley and to the small town of Hornberg. My connection to this place gave us the excuse to visit the home of the family where my guitar serenade had happened. To arrive unannounced leads easily to disappointment, and this is what we experienced on this occasion. The family had just arrived home from their holiday minutes before us. Confusion set in. We retreated for the night to a youth hostel high up on the hills of Hornberg. Next morning the head of the family picked us up in his car. The young lady, however, was not present and our visit became a formality. I could not show my friends the girl I had serenaded.

We continued our tour to the north, back home. We still had to fulfill the task of walking 70km with a 20kg backpack in one day. We worked out a route away from the main traffic that covered the required distance. That day started very early with the first glimpse of daylight. Our walk led through steep Black Forest mountain territory towards the west, away from any roads and settlements. Tall fir trees high up on the slopes watched over us four explorers. Our chosen route was very difficult. Our footgear was not the right quality for the trek and we soon developed blisters, but this did not stop us. Our shoes should have been softer and more flexible. We reached our destination of Ortenberg before dusk. Clenching our teeth helped to overcome the pain caused by our footgear. Even the 20kg backpack seemed to become heavier the longer we walked.

A castle waited for us. No other visitors had arrived on that day. Hot tea from a fireplace helped us to settle within strong stone walls for a good night's sleep. Such was the comfortable atmosphere in this castle from the Middle Ages that we entertained one another long into the night. We slept in the next morning and none of us had the desire to walk another day – the blisters on our heels had to go away first. Luckily one of our group's mothers came to drive us home in her car. We gladly accepted this lift.

What was the essence of this Black Forest walking tour? A short holiday with a different routine in daily life: Black Forest mountain air with that distinct fir tree smell; to be close to nature and its elements of sun, rain and wind; some good walking exercise; simple food; a time to rest and for observation; meeting new people; overcoming difficulties and the continuation of a learning process in a new environment. Such were our goals and we had achieved them. In short: Nothing is easier to experience than a few days of good times!

As soon as life started to improve in late 1950's, people had nothing better to do than reintroduce levels of social class. This development even infiltrated our boy scout movement. Groups were earmarked with their background being from either a primary school, a gymnasium, industry or university. Such a division did not help the common cause of the scouting movement . Individuals were expected to achieve according to their education level. An early symptom of this was demonstrated by the tumultuous events at my home-town carnival when groups of 'Indians' and 'cowboys' clashed.

The traditional German society did like to think in divisions, but a unifying force above such divisions was not ready to emerge in post-war Germany. Such circumstances encouraged youth to adjust their 'image' through further education. This is the path which I followed later.

At a first glance, this social class situation might look like healthy competition, but in reality it contributed to the end of the boy scout movement in Ettlingen.

A good friend of mine had dedicated many years of his life to saving the boy scout tradition. He wanted others to enjoy the unifying experience of boy scouts, but the conflict with the divisions was too strong and he eventually surrendered to the situation.

This friend, Bernhard, was the last strong leader to promote this good cause in our region.

Oberkochen

A work mate had recently moved to an optical manufacturing place in the Schwab Alps, not far from Stuttgart. He convinced me to follow in his footsteps, which I did.

Such a move 'killed two birds with one stone'. I gained independence from home and a new workplace environment. My new workplace was big and well organized. Many employees in my department had worked for the company in East Germany before the war. Any newcomer had to be their apprentice and work his way up the hierarchy ladder. As it turned out, I could only work under this hierarchy system for one year before tiring of the politics. I could not be the person they expected me to be.

The employees and their mates from 'over there' always managed to produce 'outstanding' results. The one who struggled on the 'losing side' was always me. "What a set-up!" I said to myself at the end of every day.

One other workmate, who was also not from 'over-there' but had worked many years with the company had tried hard to make it up the ladder through hard work. But his efforts were not rewarded because of the company politics. He was only in his forties and he worked long and hard hours. And then one night he was found dead at his job.

On my last day at this company I had an interesting discussion with my superior in his office.

He said to me: "We are happy with your performance, you do not have to leave us. But judging from your personality, this environment does not satisfy your abilities. You need a workplace where you can participate more freely and this can only be found in a smaller organisation."

Doesn't this explain everything? I agreed with my superior's comments. For my whole year of employment he had not discussed this situation with me. My superior must have gained his opinion from a distance, which is one way of obtaining a picture of a person.

This year also provided me with some positive outcomes. The hostel where I shared a furnished room with an apprentice provided some community initiatives with the support of the company.

I also spent time with the local athletics club after work and enjoyed success in long jump and sprint races. It was good to share interests with like-minded sports companions.

During the year I decided to leave the hostel after a corruption scandal shook the hostel management. Many borders decided to leave and look for alternative accommodation. The only other option in the small town was accommodation in private houses. I managed fairly quickly to get a room in a house with a family. In recent years, many families had built on to their homes to gain extra income from rented rooms. Here I thought I could gain an insight into the way of life of a Schwab family. I also believed that I was reasonably tidy and organised, but the lady of the house tried to teach me a different lesson.

It became quite obvious to everybody entering this house that everything was kept spotlessly clean and in a strict order. The door to the living room remained shut – only through the door window could you see that the furnishings were all covered in white sheets to keep dust off.

The lady of the house was always there to welcome her borders into the house. Every time somebody entered or left the house she never failed to welcome or farewell you with one hand while the other hand was polishing the floor behind her.

No matter how well I cleaned my room, she always gave it the final touch. One weekend I went away and did not have the time to do my personal washing. I decided to hide these clothes on the top of the wardrobe. When I returned, I found these clothes freshly washed and ironed and placed on my table.

My whole room was filled with the smell of air freshener. I headed straight into town to buy a bunch of flowers. I returned to my accommodation and met the landlady in the corridor. The flowers made her to forget my failure to comply with her idea of cleanliness. I realised I had more to learn about living in Schwab country.

The proverbial progress of the Schwab people can be traced back to their high degree of discipline towards cleanliness and order. Sometimes strong attitudes like this create an intolerance towards people with different social customs. Everything comes also with a price tag – even success. We can't have it all.

During that time in Oberkochen I bought my first car. Myself and a friend went to a car dealership in a small town near Stuttgart. The car dealer had advertised in the local paper a small car with a price tag that met my budget. As a proud owner of a Fiat-500 we left with an assurance that the car should please us. I paid cash for the car which was standard practice that time.

Our first trip on that Saturday took us to Heidelberg on a beautiful sunny day. This is when we experienced our first near-accident. We cruised over a bridge across the river Neckar, which overlooked the romantic area of old Heidelberg. We were not paying attention to the traffic lights at the end of the bridge. The lights changed to red and all the cars in front of us slowed down. I suddenly saw the star emblem of a big Mercedes in front of us. I knew I could not stop in time, and with no-one behind us, I quickly decided to turn the car around. With my spare hand, I grabbed my friend who was sitting beside me to prevent him from falling out of the car.

I turned the car around 180 degrees with only two wheels on the ground. It was a lucky escape.

We also planned to visit our home town of Ettlingen before returning to work in Oberkochen. It was during this drive that we also had another near-miss. As we were slowly driving up a long steep section of the Autobahn near Pforzheim, a truck in front of me lost its trailer. The trailer started to come towards me and then changed its course just before hitting me. It plunged through the centre-barriers of the Autobahn, careered across the oncoming lanes and smashed through the railing of the bridge and fell just short of the railway line. Everybody had a lucky escape. The truck driver, however, continued on his journey unaware that he had lost his trailer.

Rarely only one mishap occurs, there is often one to follow! Some time later, when my car was experiencing engine failure,

I contacted the car dealer for warranty service. He quickly referred me to the fine print in the contract and refused to repair my engine. This proud first-time vehicle owner had learned another lesson.

I started to fix the engine myself and also gave the car a new paint job to get it ready for sale. My work paid off with a quick sale and a healthy profit.

For the time being I decided not to have another vehicle. Oberkochen was surrounded by the Schwab Alps. The hills boasted a dense growth of mixed forests and were an ideal environment for walking tours. During the winter months the ski jumps on the slopes above the small town attracted lots of people. I tried ski jumping and had varied success. My ski outfit was not exactly the right one and limited my progress from the start. But this didn't really matter as I enjoyed the company of sport mates even, when I could not match their ski-jumping skills.

All these activities during my leisure time helped to recharge my batteries for the working week.

At this time I became disillusioned with my income at work as my wages just covered my cost of living. I had to save all year to buy a camera. I was not happy with that situation and knew things had to change. I was 21 at the time and decided that I should gain more education to enjoy a better-paying career. My new course was set and I resigned from the company and gained a new job at the company in my home town where I had performed the practical tests at the end of my apprenticeship.

Southern France

Let me now describe another excursion that led me and my friend, Harro, to Southern France. Our luggage included camping equipment and a folding canoe. We caught the train south into Switzerland and arrived in Geneva in the middle of the night. Where were we going to spend the night? A hotel booking did not even exist in our wildest dreams. So we drew on our boy scouts experience. A boy scout always finds an answer in nature. The park opposite the railway station was our solution. There was a dense magnolia bush in the middle of a big traffic island and this became our ' hotel '. All we had to do was roll out our sleeping bags. Summer helped to keep away the cold of the night.

Next morning we woke early. The busy traffic around us reminded us to move on. People rushing by on the pavements could not see us in our hide-out. A nearby fountain helped us to freshen up and get our day started almost normally.

The canoe parts fitted in each of our backpacks so we could walk through the city quite easily. On the way we negotiated in French to buy milk, bread, Swiss chocolate and fruit.

Start of river Rhone

Our first destination lay outside the city, where the river Rhone runs out of Lake Geneva and begins its long run towards the Mediterranean in the south. Narrow passages mark the start of the Rhone valley. After the first river barrage, the valley opens up into more open country. Here we found a suitable riverbank to launch our canoe. Summer turned out quite hot under clear skies. Once we were in the boat with our luggage, life became for us the special break we had wanted.

This first part of the river presented an unspoilt natural course – ships could not travel here. For a number of days we were alone on the river. During the day we canoed downstream, the heat of the summer limiting our activity on the water. Long before dusk we looked usually for an anchor point. Small islands in the river became our preferred places to erect our tent and cook a meal on a fire from branches washed onshore. Maintaining the canoe, catching fish with provisional gear, reading and playing our guitars were our nightly entertainments, before we had to take refuge from the mosquitoes. To keep the majority of mosquitoes away from us, we had to keep our small tent closed, but this did not help us beat the heat at all.

Boating on upper river Rhone

As a matter of fact, we did not get much sleep during our days along the river. The morning sun made the mosquito night-invaders disappear together with most of our sleeplessness. Our lonely days on the river were still beautiful. We saw green slopes on both sides of the riverbanks, leafy woods, vineyards in the distance and no towns in sight until we arrived in Lyon. In this major city, the banks of the river were built with uniformed rock walls where small ships could anchor.

To get off the water we had to find a boat ramp. We mixed with the locals along the shore for a few hours, always keeping our canoe in our sights. We decided to leave Lyon and paddle well into the night to get out of this big city. That night, by torchlight, we found a peach orchard to camp in and pitched our tent on the side of a dirt road.

At first daylight, a farmer arrived with his tractor. We were not sure of his reception, but our reservations became unfounded when the farmer welcomed us in a friendly way. "Pick the peaches for your own consumption completely with the stem and don't break any branches, there are more than enough for me to harvest," he said. The peaches were indeed delicious: ripened in the trees, large in size, their skin yellow-red and so juicy that a bite could not contain all the juice.

The further south we paddled, the larger the river Rhone grew. More and more barrages regulated the shipping traffic through their sluices. We were not allowed to pass through these barrages with the ships, because our canoe was by far too small to withstand the moving masses of water in a sluice. The old river bed with its reduced water flow allowed our boat to drift around the man-made river barrages. As soon as we were back on the main river, we had to respect the shipping traffic again.

Here, in the middle of summer, a strong wind blew every afternoon from the south. They call this wind 'Sirocco'. These strong winds originate from as far as the Sahara in North Africa. They blow hot, dry air straight up river Rhone to the north. Some days the Sirocco wind blew so intensely that big waves formed on wide river surfaces. At these times we had to leave the river and wait on its banks until the ferocity of this wind died down before dusk.

When we paddled into the city of Montelimar I began to feel sick. Was it the consumption of too many peaches? Colic-like symptoms in my abdomen forced me to pay an urgent visit to the local hospital. They put me straight on the table in the operating theatre, but the surgeon could not find what was wrong with me. They admitted me to hospital for observation for the next five days. It proved a perfect opportunity for me to practice my French. Only then questions about my status of employment and insurance were raised, everybody was friendly and helpful.

Montelimar on river Rhone

Sometimes, when you see a dentist or a doctor, the pain disappears for some reason. This happened on this occasion and I joined my patient friend in our tent on the riverbank. Everything seemed to be back to normal, so we continued our canoe tour.

As a marginal note, I was examined by a number of medical professionals over the next six years before it was properly diagnosed that I had appendicitis. In the end I only just survived this old appendix with its tumour. However my health problems did not affect me again for the duration of our canoe excursion.

Places in the south of France like Orange and Avignon invited us into ancient Roman history with their temples, amphitheatres, fortresses and triumphal arches surrounding pulsing modern city life. People live here in harmony with ancient history. As a result of such a continued tradition, people are very tolerant which is typical for this area of Southern France.

We embarked in Avignon from the river Rhone for good and put our canoe back into two backpacks. From now on we continued our excursion by local buses and on foot.

The Southern part of France in the triangle between Avignon, Marseille and Montpellier is called La Camargue and this is where different cultures had left their footprints during history.

Vast grasslands hug the river Rhone on its journey to the Mediterranean. The tiny fishing township of St Marie De La Mer, right on the coast of this Rhone delta, became our final destination. On our way we visited also a bull farm that supplied bulls for fights in arenas of Arles and Nimes. It was here that we were told that the main bullfight of the year will be staged in the ancient arena of Nimes in 10 days time. This was a spectacle we had to see!

We explored this region of La Camargue on foot and pitched our tent with most of our luggage on a high point of the beach. There was no-one else around with the exception of only a few local fishermen. They reassured us that our tent would be left alone while we were away.

One should try to imagine something like this in today's world of 2007.

Les Baux, Southern France

Each time we returned to our tent on the beach, even after more than one day's absence, we found everything in good order. What a great experience with such good people.

A trip by bus and on foot brought us through Arles, Tarascon to St. Remy De Province, a little-known historical region at the foothills of the Alps. Ancient civilisations conquered this strategic 'aerie-of-an-eagle' to reign over this part of the La Camargue. Celtic, Greek and Roman architecture were present here. Well-preserved triumphal arches bore testament to the Roman presence in the lower fields of the area and the ruins of Les Beaux on a rock peak were the remains from battles to gain control of this strategic location.

The area also boasts a number of more recent buildings. One, in particular, had its windows barred. This was the building where the artist Van Gogh spent the last years of his life in solitary confinement after cutting off his ear out of desperation. He later committed suicide.

I looked through this small window in the Van Gogh cell to gain an impression of the view that might have contributed to the artist's strange behaviour. What I saw was a field of dried yellow grass climbing up a slope – this did not turn me insane!

During our stay we were completely on our own – no curious, busy tourists in sight. Rich cultured flower fields bordered both sides of the road on our return to Tarascon. What a welcome diversion from the dry landscape and the summer heat we had left behind us. How water can transform a landscape with a helping hand!

Arriving back on our beach in St Marie De La Mer, our tent was still intact. We allowed a day for relaxation on the beach before more exploring.

Another trip took us west to Aigue Mortes, a fortress surrounded completely by deep-water trenches. Only one folding bridge allowed access into the massive stone walls with its observation towers on the corners. Over the centuries many civilizations had built here – the Gauls, Romans, West Goths and the Franks had all left their marks in

Aigues Mortes. During the 16th and 17th centuries this fortress became a refuge for the Huguenots (Protestants in a mainly catholic France).

Later in the afternoon, a bus took us back to Arles. After sunset, we found ourselves a fair distance away from our beach camp so we decided to spend some hours of this night in a small restaurant with a cup of tea in front of us. It was a Sunday and the whole family of the restaurant had gathered for a big, long dinner. We watched this family dinner where all age groups were represented. There was lots of talk and laughter, endless courses and plenty of wine. The initial festive table became a pile of dishes as the evening wore on and people were singing well into the early hours of Monday.

The patroness came to see us occasionally asking: "Do you want something else besides your cup of tea?" Again later she raised this question: "Are you all right, is there anything else you need?" We had to admit that we had left it too late to get back to our home on the beach. Straight away she said: "My sons have cleared their room for you tonight. You have to get up before six o'clock, when our bakery starts making French sticks. Our customers only accept them hot." She said that after six o'clock she wouldn't have any time for us. Tired as we were, we fell straight asleep under the gables of the house in beds with thick blankets and large pillows. At six o'clock sharp we got the wake up call.

We found it more than appropriate to say thank you before our departure from these friendly people. We were asked to perform not only one song but many more with our guitars. A constantly growing audience joined in from the road – the customers watched while they bought their French sticks. We exchanged songs and wine was served again. All this took place in the bakery while staff looked after the French sticks in the oven. Long after everything was sold out, we finally decided to move on. The new day had already passed midday. These friendly people with a great understanding and a helping hand for others had found time besides their daily work to share pleasure with others.

The end of the month drew closer. We had to direct ourselves towards Nimes without delay to see the bullfight.

The next day we caught a local bus to the event. The ancient arena could not be missed, its fabulous architecture stood out in the city centre. It is the best-preserved arena dating back to Roman rule. The arena was still hosting big events like the final bullfight of the year drawing crowds of spectators, filling the arena.

As we arrived more than one day before this event, we purchased our tickets straight away to make sure we did not miss out.

We had ample time to explore the area before the bullfight. Near the arena was an open, wide park featuring an old observatory on top of a hill. This building dated back to Roman occupation. The solid stone building with its dome was closed to the public.

There was an aqueduct not far from the city, which spanned the river Guard. The river wends its way here through massive boulders of rock – the high arches of the aqueduct span across this river valley. This aqueduct was built during the Roman occupation to supply Nimes with water from out of the surrounding mountain region of Ardeche. Every past culture had to deal with a shortage of water, so this Roman aquaduct was a genius solution – and is still used today! History has demonstrated that a quality water supply in most cases determined the life span of a civilisation. It is about time we took heed of this message.

Nimes: Sunday, August 30, 1964, 4pm. A full arena awaited the major bullfight of the year. The sun still reached most parts of the circular arena oval, where a colourful spectacle had started.

The arena's astonishing architecture features arches of solid rock. The further these circles go out, the higher the arches stack up on top of one another to support the climbing steps of the inner arena. Ice creams and drinks were served between the rows of spectators. Music filled the air. All this stopped when fanfares announced the beginning of the spectacle.

Bull-fight opening in Roman amphitheatre, Nimes

All participants in the bullfight rallied on the well protected floor of the arena in a colourful display. The bull was then released into the arena followed by loud calls from the public. The fight in Nimes follows the Spanish rules. Assistants emerge from behind secure walls, one at the time, with the red 'capa' to provoke the bull, which was running from one red 'capa' to the other in an outer circle of the arena field. Then the 'picador' arrived on a horse and planted a number of colourful small spears into the bull's body, avoiding the bull's run with his highly-skilled movements. The crowd became louder and got up more frequently on their feet. Banderillas joined the picador to confuse the bull even more. The bull steamed through the arena, leaving dust clouds behind him. The torero appeared from behind safety walls to join in the dramatic race with the bull.

A torero starts his display with a slow build-up so the bull does not collapse from his wounds too early.

Once the bull came within a hair's breath of gouging the torero on his horse. The spectators nearly went nuts. The torero weakened the bull with knife stabbings and the bull came down on his front legs. The matador used a sword to deliver a death blow to the bull. One bullfight was over. The dead bull was pulled out of the arena with a tractor. Other bullfights followed with different outcomes. It is rare that either the torero or the matador is picked up by the bull and very badly injured or killed.

The whole spectacle of a bullfight bears a mark of brutality, but bullfights have for centuries been a cultural expression in Spain, Portugal and France. Spain even exported the bullfight to its colonies. The real bullfights were held mainly in Valencia in Spain and here in Nimes.

Only those who have witnessed a bullfight can join an informed discussion on the brutality of such a custom. The cultural claims in such a discussion are that the bull and the torero have equal chances in the event which serves mainly to excite spectators. The spectators' support changes constantly from the bull to the torero. Having seen other bullfights in Spain, I can say this bullfight in Nimes was the most impressive one.

The history of bullfights goes back 2000 years when gladiators fought in Rome to satisfy people's desire for excitement and to divert them from political realities. Fights with lions or bulls were common. For the bull fighter the stakes were high – he was fighting for his freedom, no matter what the reasons were for his imprisonment.

Against this background, bullfights in the early 1960s were relatively civilised with their rules. This fact, however, did not stop public opinion moving against such displays of brutality. Today, in 2007, most bullfights are outlawed.

Bullfights divided the opinion of the spectators, their encouragement shifting constantly from the bull to the torero. The spectators were excited, disappointed, made bets, laughed, shouted and hurled abuse. All this was the essence of the atmosphere of a bullfight. One distinct difference emerged at the end of a bullfight though. Everybody, without exception, felt respect for the defeated bull. This respect didn't apply to the torero, when a bull defeated him. The whole arena turned crazy then.

During a number of bullfights, the best-known torero usually raises the expectations of the crowd. He has to deliver a good performance or the crowd will turn against him. It was here in Nimes that we saw our first bullfight. We tried to capture the atmosphere with the people and this became an exceptional experience for us. It cannot be denied that bullfights have been a vital expression of the people here. When they face a fight between life and death in an arena, hope for life gains strength.

The bullfight was the highlight of our tour of Southern France.

After the bullfight, we only had a few days left to get back home. In order to hitch-hike, we sent our boat and tent home via train.

Leaving the beach of St Marie De La Mer we experienced a very different way of travelling along the roads of Southern France. We hitch-hiked because we simply could not afford any other means of travelling.

Hitch-hiking was still reasonably safe in those days – positive encounters outweighed negative ones. In most cases, when people stopped they were prepared to lend a helping hand. This view has changed completely today where hitch-hiking is more likely to end up in a possible crime scene. This is a fact and should be accepted. The world has changed.

As youngsters we seek new activities and experiences and learn from them. As boy scouts in uniform we used this transport quite often in the past. Hitch-hiking was common in the boy-scout culture of England, where this scouting movement started. In Germany, we adopted many customs from there. A boy scout in a tidy uniform usually received privileged attention from the general public. Hitch-hiking could connect people who might never have met. I remember many friendly and interesting encounters during my hitch-hiking years. I also must admit that there were some risky encounters as we experienced on our return trip from Southern France.

A few lifts on the busy Rhone highway brought us back to the city of Lyon in less than two days. In one incident we got out of a car in the city centre at the traffic lights. Before the lights changed from red to green, the driver of a red sports car indicated for us to join him. We sat in the back, explaining to our fashionably dressed driver where we wanted to go. He surged his way through the traffic at high speed – well above the city speed limit.

A queue of cars in all lanes forced him to stop in front of another set of traffic lights. Our suspicions were raised. I looked at my friend and just when the line of cars started to move we both jumped over the edge of the cabriolet door on to the road, avoiding passing cars. Our driver didn't make an attempt to stop. As soon as the traffic allowed us to reach the footpath, a police car stopped in front of us.

A number of officers got out of the car and approached us. They asked us to join them in their car for an interrogation at police headquarters. We had no idea what was going on and were subjected to a thorough investigation. Our backpacks were searched. Questions were asked in relation to our journey.

It was only late that night when the police confirmed our identity and the investigation came to an end. Surprisingly, we received an apology for being under police detention for so long. We asked why we were detained and the police responded with quite a dramatic explanation: "The driver of the red sports cabriolet is under strong suspicion of having shot and robbed a hitch-hiker in the outskirts of the city only half an hour before we picked you up. You could easily have become his next target if you hadn't made your escape."

As it was late at night by this stage, the police made a generous offer to put us up at a luxury hotel for the night. The bookings had already been made and the police drove us to the hotel. A fantastic night's sleep awaited us in total luxury.

Television and a mini-bar in our suite kept us awake for a while. We had to make the most of this luxurious atmosphere. We woke early to bright daylight. Wasn't this a gentlemanly French police action!

We were also given the advice to stop hitch-hiking in the area of Lyon, for a very good reason.

We were a bit short of funds to pay the railway for the remaining distance back home. We phoned home and had some money wired to us so that we could board a train to get us out of Lyon.

After arriving at home, the reality of life caught up with me the next day.

I had to be back at work, whereas my friend had another week of holidays before his studies began.

Our five-week holiday was blessed with summer sunshine – not one drop of rain. The rain started when we got home!

Our excursion to France taught us to communicate with their people. Learning a foreign language while on the road in that country is far more successful than school lessons. We learned from the people how they live, work and enjoy life.

New Horizons – Work Life, Studies

Matriculation

As well as working, I attended night classes in the nearby town of Karlsruhe to prepare for matriculation.

My days were packed with duties because I wanted to advance myself for the years to come. During the day I worked in my profession, at night I found myself back on the school bench. The difference now was that this was my choice, not an obligation. The same applied to the teachers who were committed to advancing a group of professional people through further education. This further education towards matriculation opened possibilities that could not otherwise be considered.

The teachers were quite different in their approach from those at the gymnasium. They lectured in their field with a real commitment towards the students who were making a nightly effort to learn and to achieve.

The teachers and students had similar goals. The teachers worked the extra nights to earn some extra income. The students paid their fees expecting quality teaching, that would improve their educational and career prospects.

The 12 students in our night class came from different backgrounds: industry, research, the airforce, public service, education and finance. We all asked questions pertaining to our different fields of interest.

This way we all learned from this free flow of information – even the teachers.

What would our higher education institutions be like if their students came from the 'real world' with their own specific knowledge? The level of achievements would be so much higher. Most students instead hang on to the 'old school bench' and 'study life' from there. We haven't come that far since school was 'invented'. If we had a system where work flows into education, and not the other way around, an individual could stay in close contact with a work environment and could progress through professional and educational levels while in that job. To my knowledge, a number of renowned companies have very successfully adopted this approach.

Our French teacher only spoke French to us – a quite realistic approach in teaching a language. He used a very simple vocabulary and when it came to an explanation he also used mimicry, hand signals and diagrams on the blackboard.

This was not the case with my English teacher. He kept to the book and tested students on who could best recall a page, a sentence or the exact wording of a rule. I found this to be a rather stupid approach. Was this the reason my English marks were less positive than my French results? Our world is a funny place, teachers are not excluded.

Our class consisted of two females and 10 males. We attended classes every week night and studied on weekends. I had to ride my bicycle to attend these classes as the public transport did not suit my timetable. I thought myself lucky to be living so close to the town and could be home on the same day.

For a short time only I lived with my step-parents again. They wanted to support my efforts which I understood quite well. But this did not prove to be successful as talk of being a chemistry engineer came back again into our 'game'. I decided to stay out of it and live independently, which I did.

After three years of study, it was time for the final exams. The atmosphere was tense. There were 11 students at that stage – one female had dropped out due to tragic reasons. All the students succeeded with excellent results.

Our teachers were visibly proud of this achievement. New horizons opened for us with the matriculation certificates in our hands.

A closing ceremony took place in style on a weekend night where all the teachers celebrated with their 11 graduates. We all thanked our teachers and I performed a guitar concert interpreting Sor, Giuliani and Bach. Our final meeting was a big success. After that, we all moved in different directions in our careers and lost contact with one another.

I felt a huge relief after three very busy years. I resigned from work to do something different again and enrolled at the Ruperto Carola University of Heidelberg.

Scandinavia

With three months before the university semester started, I again had the opportunity to travel. I joined two fellow students in their car for a trip to Scandinavia.

The so-called 'birdflight route' took us across a magnificent bridge to Denmark. Flat countryside with the legendary Danish cattle welcomed us under a mixed sky. It was summer time. Nobody here complained about the heat in this part of the world.

The mainly dark, red brick homes in the countryside reminded of a similarity with Northern Germany.

The world appeared more peaceful here. People carried on their business but did not rush. The modern, clean city of Copenhagen started when houses on our route became more frequent. The rather cool weather didn't invite us to stay a day longer than necessary.

Mermaid, Copenhagen

The royal castle, built in historic solid stone, stood out from the rest of this modern city. The most common transport in Copenhagen was the bicycle. These were owned by the public. Citizens of all age groups could freely use the bicycles with only one condition – they must leave them in good order after reaching the destination. Discipline and trust allowed such a system to work.

On the city's seafront, where the harbour and airport are situated, there is a statue of a mermaid. At first glance she looked rather small. A second glance revealed her pliant form as she emerged out of the waters.

The Tivoli amusement park attracts many visitors with its spectacular light shows after sunset. Young and old flock to see this Tivoli magic.

Tivoli, Copenhagen

After our quick visit to this fine city, we continued our trip the next day on a ferry boat across the Oeresund passage to Sweden.

Today in 2007, some 40 years later, a gigantic bridge spans from Denmark to Sweden allowing road traffic between the two countries.

We decided to head for Stockholm, which was another 600km by road. The landscape changed from here onwards. Outcrops of naked rock interrupted fir forests which varied in their density across the country.

Most houses in Sweden were built in timber and coloured red with the windows and door frames a different colour.

The traffic was only heavy near the towns. The roads were lefthand drive, like in England. We had to pay more attention being used to right-hand drive traffic but we travelled through Sweden without incident. Just two years later, Sweden changed its traffic to right-hand drive. A change which would have been very difficult in other countries, if not out of question. People in colder climates exhibit a rational way of thinking, which has, over the generations, resulted also in a high standard of living.

The roads passed smooth, rock boulders dotted throughout pine forests and occasionally we got a glimpse of lake shores. Fir trees, like pine trees, even grew on top of the granite boulders but they were not as tall as those in the Black Forest.

On our way to Stockholm we passed only a few small towns.

Forests, granite boulders and lakes made up the landscape.

Scandinavia's population is less dense than other parts of Europe. Small settlements are scattered with their typical red timber houses built in open clearings in the forests. Only larger settlements form centres which feature block or concrete buildings. Here a traveller met a peaceful world. People were rather cautious towards tourists but we still enjoyed conversations.

We split up before our arrival in Stockholm and this opened new horizons for me. I gave hitch-hiking a try. Nobody wanted to give me a lift in this country which forced me to take a public transport.

The Swedish railway carried me right into the centre of Stockholm. A wide-open modern city welcomed me on a sunny, warm day. My first priority was to look for accommodation that suited my budget. Not an easy undertaking in a big foreign city! Fortunately all the people I spoke with could answer my questions quite well in English. After only a few enquiries, I found out where a youth hostel accommodation was located.

I decided to go there on foot which gave me the best opportunity of seeing the city. Waterways combined with open spaces. Outstanding buildings gave a magnificent impression: city hall, royal palaces, Skepsholmen Island with its sailing ship, the Slussen Elevator Tower.

Many roads were built high up without intersections to keep the traffic moving.

Stockholm, Sweden

Around Central Station, the underground rail was under heavy construction. Pedestrians could walk freely without the usual traffic congestion.

To my knowledge, no other European city matched Stockholm with its modern facilities and infrastructure at that time. After a few hours of sightseeing across the city, I found my accommodation in Slussen. I left my guitar and backpack in the hostel to enjoy another excursion. Wandering through the parks, I was surprised at how openly

Swedish girls sought contact with strangers like me. The language, however, caused a problem and for that reason

I could not get into a conversation.

Here in the north, daylight during summer was much longer than at home. This confused me so I looked around for somebody to confirm the time. I was on the jetty at Slussen where the ships to Finland anchored. There was a young lady walking on the jetty so I asked her for the time. She answered with a special smile which did not escape my attention. How could I know that this smile was the beginning of a romance that would last my whole life?

I also asked this charming lady: "Do you like guitar music?" She replied: "Oh yes but there is no guitar around here."

I responded: "Should I bring my guitar which I have stored at Slussen in a hostel not far from here?"

"If you wish, I wait here," she said. I ran as fast as I could to Slussen, returning to the jetty with my guitar. I was sure she would have left in the mean time. But arriving at the jetty, I was wrong. She was still there. Near our meeting point rested an old sailing ship in calm waters on the small island of Skepsholmen. A nice pedestrian crossing led us to the island. Next to the sailing ship there was a green slope, where we sat down. For over an hour I sang and played my guitar. Brilliant sunshine accompanied us.

She said: "I enjoyed our meeting very much."

It was time to part ways. We said goodbye and I gave her my business card. Then she told that she was leaving the next night on the ship to Finland.

I walked back to my accommodation, the sun set on the horizon just before 11pm. I doubted I would hear from the young lady from Finland again.

Next morning the weather had a surprise for me. The sunny weather turned nasty. It was cold, rainy and windy.

I took a bus out of the city in pouring rain. It was impossible to see the girl from Finland again. A couple of years later she told me: "I was looking for you, before my ship departed."

One day sunshine, next day miserable. That's life!

A long-lasting romance had begun here, yet I had no clue about it.

I tried hitch-hiking again but it was heavy rain and a passing car gave me a complete dirt shower. That was enough. A bus took me back to the central railway station, where I caught a train across Sweden to the west into Norway where I hoped to find better weather. My train moved slowly and there were few passengers on board. The landscape repeated itself with granite boulders, forests, hamlets and lakes.

The train stopped frequently but more people watched than boarded. The train stopped at the Norwegian border. I was, by then, its only passenger and walked across the border after showing my passport.

I tried hitch-hiking the short distance to Oslo. A car did stop for me but the driver told me to get out when he realised I was not a local. So I had no choice but to take a bus to the city centre, just before nightfall.

On my way to the youth hostel, I stumbled across a few strange characters. There were completely drunk women who had nothing better to do than bump into me. (Alcohol also plays its role in this part of the world).

Luck must have been on my side as the youth hostel accepted my request for accommodation, even though it was so late at night.

The next morning I wanted to explore the city and its surroundings. The weather was a mixed bag: very little sunshine, heavy clouds and showers. It was rather cold, despite it being summer. I still went ahead and explored the city paying visits to the Munk Art Museum, the Viking Museum with its historical ship and the ski-jump facility at Holmenkollen, which had mountain slopes covered with forests to the north of the city. Everywhere I went.

I was mostly on my own. Everybody else must have been at work or indoors because of the poor weather conditions. It was only towards the evening that more people came out and gathered around bars.

Holmenkollen, Oslo, Norway

On my way to Holmenkollen, I gained a superb view over the city's harbour where a bay stretches far out into the sea. Small islands in the bay broke the silvery gleam in the water, which changed constantly as the sun broke through the heavily-clouded sky. This spectacle of nature gave me a first impression of what the fjords looked like further north in Norway.

Viking-ship, Oslo, Norway

I decided to go home because of the poor weather and because I was not able to make any contacts here with the locals.

A shipping passage back to Denmark would prove the perfect end to a well-rounded journey. There was no shortage of places on board the ship that embarked the next morning.

The ship left Oslo affording a magnificent view of the city and its surroundings embraced in a half circle of mountains and forests. This view remains my best memory from my short visit to Norway.

The ship was bound for Copenhagen without any stopovers. The passage led through Skagerrak into Kattegat – both sea passages from the North Sea to the Baltic Sea are known for their stormy nature. However, we did not encounter such conditions, our voyage was calm and quite pleasant.

I met some nice people on the ship and their company helped pass the time. They asked me to play guitar for them. It is amazing how music unites people. Such an experience confirmed my beliefs that a guitar is a very good way to connect to others. Music is a language that everybody understands.

When we arrived in Copenhagen the next morning, one of the passengers offered me to join him in his car to Southern Germany. His destination was France. This offer not only saw me home to my doorstep, but also gave me a chance to further practise my French.

Leaving the routine of life and travelling, helped young people like myself to better understand and deal with people from different backgrounds. The more we see, the more we can learn. Life is by far our best teacher. An isolated formal education has its limits.

Tour Eiffel – Paris

Paris is always worth it

On board the ship from Oslo, I formed an acquaintance with a Norwegian couple, who were on their way to Paris. They suggested we could meet in Paris and I could be an interpreter for them. With this in mind, I took the train from Heidelberg to Paris only a few days after arriving home from Scandinavia.

On the train, I must have sat in the wrong compartment section. A big gentleman and his travelling companion, an attractive woman, were obviously not happy that I had joined their compartment. At first I did my best reading a magazine and not being in their way.

When the ticket inspector arrived, he informed me I was in the first-class section but only had a second-class ticket. He gave me a hefty fine even though I admitted my mistake and offered to move to the right compartment. The fine allowed me to stay in the first class apartment, but had seriously dented my limited budget. The fast French train arrived on time in the Gare Du Nord in Paris.

My meeting with the Norwegian couple failed to eventuate which did not completely surprise me. Anyway, I decided to make my short time in Paris worthwhile. I found a youth hostel with affordable beds and spent the day sightseeing.

It was after that first night, I realised that sophisticated thieves mixed in the population and were not adverse to robbing youth hostel guests. My new electric shaver disappeared from under my pillow that night. Now how could I maintain my image in Paris?

Near the hostel was a pet cemetery – a typical French institution. People in Paris must love their pets. They remember them with marble graves, pet statues and pictures behind glass designs.

The more we move away from nature, the more we are in search for something closer to nature like a pet.

The next day I also visited Montmartre, the Champs Elysees, the Louvre, Place de la Concorde with the Egyptian obelisk, Notre Dame, the Arc de Triumph, L'Opera, Dome des Invalides, Les Tuileries and St German – the artists' quarter.

I also paid a visit to a typical Paris parfumerie. Even a small customer like myself received a special reception with a great variety of perfumes been tested on my hands, while I sat patiently. A charming lady went through the ritual of applying a drop of 'flacon a parfum' on my hands while explaining their special qualities. She said the perfumes reminded people of nature which seemed to be lost in a big city like Paris. I ended up with a small scent bottle that bore the smell of orchids from the El Faiyum cultivations in Egypt. The smell was overwhelming and so was the price for a few drops in a special bottle.

(Much later on, this perfume was destined to be sent all the way to Finland as a thank you to Arja, my friend from the jetty, for sending me a letter.)

During my short stay in Paris, I also found time to visit the Moulin-Rouge. I did this without having to buy champagne – the expensive ticket for entertainment with a woman in that famous establishment.

There were not many pornographic movies around in 1965. The Moulin Rouge establishment offered an insight into a sexual world which was not commonly known in societies of this era.

Moulin Rouge, Paris

I ended my visit to Paris with a trip to nearby Versailles using the underground and above-ground railway systems.

The underground in Paris is the best way to move around in this big city. It reflects French ingenuity as they had designed the trains for efficient service. The trains run on special rubber profiled wheels which means that not only do they give the carriages a smooth ride, but the wheels do not wear out the train lines as metal wheels do. They just replace the rubber-profile wheels when they wear down.

Arriving in Versailles in 1965, you found fruit and vegetable markets where fresh, well-priced produce from the local farms was displayed on long tables. I bought beautiful peaches and grapes for a very good price.

These markets were under a row of big elm trees and situated just before the entrance to the Versailles palace and its vast gardens laid out in a geometric design.

When I visited Versailles on a much later occasion, I saw how the surroundings had dramatically changed from an agricultural suburb of Paris to a tourist centre in its own right.

It is easy to see why Paris attracts such big numbers of tourists.

Paris is always worth a visit.

Artist at work, Paris

It was time to leave Paris, so I hitch-hiked back to Heidelberg.

Heidelberg

Daily life and its routines started for me in Heidelberg. A friend of mine who was already at university gave me accommodation for a couple of days so that I could organize my enrolment at Ruperto Carola University studying sports, medicine and French. It was a few weeks before lectures began. I was quick to apply for a job in my profession in the company of my apprenticeship in order to get hold of more funds for my studies. In 1965 universities in Germany charged student fees per semester and students had to supply most of the materials themselves. In other words, further education was quite expensive at that time. I did my best to prepare myself for this new step.

When further education later became more popular, resources were directed into politically-motivated short gains without much regard towards quality standards. I had heard many professors complaining about the poor standard of school–leavers entering universities. The universities were profit-driven. We rarely see past the length of our nose!

I could not count on any financial support from home. "You are on your own if you don't do what I tell you," my step-father said. The change in generations is as old as human society.

I had to prove German citizenship at university but unfortunately, because of my adoption, my existence as a citizen was neglected. All of a sudden I found myself stateless.

Germany is probably the only country in the world where citizenship is not proven through a passport – this must be a remnant from the thinking of the 'Third Reich'.

Anyway, I had to remind my step-parents of their civil obligations. Like my adoption, they agreed to make my citizenship legal. The law made parents responsible for the maintenance of their children's education. When I applied for a scholarship based on performance, this was rejected because the taxation authorities had to supply information on the wealth status of my step-parents. They earned too much money for me to be eligible for a scholarship. I was officially told to take my parents to court but that was something I would never do – I owed them at least respect.

I decided, none-the-less, to give it a go at the university. I managed to earn good money to support my goals.

When I did not live at home, I did visit my step-parents from time to time which helped our relationship. On a visit not long after returning from Scandinavia, mum handed me a letter with her comments: "You have a letter from Finland." This letter gave me quite a surprise, because I never thought this Finnish girl from Stockholm would write to me. It was indeed her letter! It had only a few words: "Can you remember me from Stockholm? My name is Arja. I am looking forward to hearing from you. Here is my address and thank you for your guitar concert."

A keen correspondence began between Finland and Germany communicating in English. Romance apart, there were priorities to tackle one step at time. The remaining six weeks of work turned out to be quite interesting. The company gave me a special task which involved the set-up of an automated dividing head on a production machine. I had to design, install, set up control functions and perform a test run. I performed this task to everybody's satisfaction and was given a very substantial bonus. I knew this company would provide a good opportunity of an income during my semester breaks.

Back in Heidelberg, my usual student life started. I was finding it hard to find accommodation. One of the reasons was the presence of American military personnel, who had high subsidies to live outside the military barracks. Students could not match these rates. Heidelberg also became a centre for Americans to be sent to Vietnam. Their presence affected everybody's life. Daily incidents in the public saw regular arrests.

Despite all this, I found the room in a private house which gave me a roof over my head, a bed, table, chair and wardrobe . All my possessions fitted into one suitcase, plus my guitar.

German universities recommended guidelines for studies – every student has to have a study plan. This taught students self-discipline – a skill they also needed in their life after studies.

Generally students had more free time than working people. A student is master of his timetable and how he spends his time is his own responsibility. Many were tempted to lose focus on priorities. This liberal environment sometimes makes university appear 'luxury' institutions. There was a large number of students living in this environment for the sake of a liberal lifestyle, away from the daily pressure which the majority of society had to bear.

I have a friend who studied for 14 years. He had found his niche away from the 'real world'.

Meanwhile, my first semester passed very well and so did my funds. I had to use my break to earn money again.

Finland visit

Before this was going to happen, it crossed my mind to visit Arja in Finland. Winter reigned over Scandinavia. The railway took me to Stockholm in Sweden and from there on boat to Finland. This winter happened to be the most severe one since the war. The train had a snow plough mounted on the front to push the snow off the rails. The snow sprayed into the air. Nothing could be seen through the windows in this 'snow storm'. The snow also came through the closed windows into all carriages and the heating failed completely. The temperature fell to minus 30 degree Celsius during the night. These German trains were not built to stand such extreme cold.

In Stockholm I changed to the ship in Slussen. The sea was frozen solid all over Stockholm. The sea passage to Helsinki was closed from the ice. The only open passage to Finland was maintained by Finnish icebreakers to the city of Turku (also known by the Swedish name of Abo). One icebreaker steamed in front of our ship, but our ship still shifted ice masses with her bow. The ice rushed along both sides with a spectacular noise. The whole ship vibrated, when she hit new ice. Our ship pushed herself constantly onto the ice islands making them to disappear under her weight with a tremendous bang. It is amazing how technology can deal with nature's forces in an extreme winter. During the day the Baltic Sea offered a view of an icy wilderness with waves stopped in their movements and shaped in ice.

Ice-breaker in the Baltic Sea

At midnight our ship anchored on the islands of Ahvenanmaa, Swedish Aland – halfway between Stockholm and Turku. Our ship entered these islands on Finnish territory. Reflections from the snow lit the darkness of the night. It was snowing. The fir tree forest loaded with snow lined both sides of the ship. This gave the impression that we were driving high up on land through a forest.

A passage through the archipelagos of South-west Finland is one of the most beautiful sea passages in the world. Winter, like summer, has its special features. In summer this passage takes place under the midnight sun highlighting these many islands with their granite outcrops and their never-retreating fir tree vegetation on top. The dark-red-sun light on the horizon dips this summer scenery into a fairytale world. I experienced such a summer passage a couple of times in later years.

Winter had imposed total silence. The passengers were relaxed. They trusted the ship to do this hard work and expressed their relaxation, often under the influence of alcohol, by becoming amorous with members of the opposite sex. Our ship became a sheer love boat. This was not the case on the return trip to Sweden. The atmosphere was very different – passengers were more reserved and kept to themselves.

The ship arrived in the early morning hours through another archipelago leading to Turku. A real winter welcomed me here:

Frozen seawater, snow-covered land, roads, house roofs, the sky closed in with more snow on the way. North-west on a slope behind the harbour, I could see the towers of an old stone-built castle and, a bit further to the north, the pointed tower of the cathedral.

I did not expect anyone to meet me at the harbour. I caught a taxi to Arja's house but nobody answered the door bell. I was disappointed. I left a bunch of red carnations with a note at the door and returned to the city on foot to arrange affordable accommodation.

In general people understood English, so I was spared the exercise in Finnish, which was a completely new language for me. It is a hard language to understand. The language is best learned by talking to people as text books only bring confusion when it comes to all the vowels in well-extended words. For instance, 'good day' in Finnish is 'hyvaa paivaa'. Nobody ever could guess it.

The Finnish language has survived in relative isolation over many centuries. The language constitutes the backbone of survival for the Finnish people during foreign occupation by Sweden and Russia.

A source for the Finnish language can be traced back to Hokaido in northern Japan. Many years later, I discovered that the native population in Hawaii share many similar words with Finnish and Japanese languages. These words are mainly to do with hunting, fishing and boating, which indicates a link in ancient migrations.

Meanwhile, from my accommodation in the city I telephoned Arja without success. I only had three days in Finland. The next day I went to her house again. The flowers were gone which told me I was welcome. I was in luck, Arja was there.

I tried to communicate using a mix of English and Finnish words but this only brought a big smile to people's faces.

On a Finnish table there is dark rye bread, fish, potatoes, milk, meat – all in different varieties. A beer is also quite common. The only alcohol was available at the 'viinakortti', which was later abolished in 1969.

My cold winter day was best spent indoor sightseeing so I visited some museums exhibiting mainly Finnish art and history. I also saw the old castle near the harbour and the cathedral in town. In the evening Arja and I visited a cinema screening the James Bond movie 'The Thunder Ball'. Arja's sister and her friend kept

a curious eye on us from behind. Everything was covered in snow outside. Traffic in the city moved as if the road was dry. No wonder Finland supplies the best rally drivers in the world.

The wind made life outside very unpleasant -nose, ears, cheeks had to be protected from frostbite. I had never experienced such cold conditions.

The houses are built to keep the heated air inside and use special double windows. Only older houses were built from timber. Newer houses were constructed in concrete blocks incorporating insulation materials. During the long winter people stay mostly indoors. Furnishings are generally of a very high standard in a typical style of Scandinavian simplicity.

Summer arrives here with its long daylight only for a short time. Many leave the city for their summer cottages on sea or lake shores.

Finnish sauna

Whether it is winter or summer, the Finnish sauna is an institution throughout the entire year. No visitor escapes from this experience because a sauna is an ancient cultural element of the Finnish society.

In times where today's facilities did not exist, Finnish sauna served many purposes: stocking up the body with heat, achieving a thorough cleaning of the whole body, creating a sterile environment for births, for healing, and last but not least, a place to relax .

A sauna is built out of Finnish timbers. Stepped benches allow heat absorption in front of a heated oven which receives, from time to time, a ladle of water to intensify the heat. A bundle of birch twigs punishes the body for better blood circulation and water from a bucket or shower assists the cleaning process. This cycle can be repeated as often as you like.

Some go to the extreme and move from the sauna straight into snow or even swim in an icy waterhole. When you survive this, you know you are in good health. A good drink after a sauna helps to restore moisture levels. Sauna has conquered the whole world. A sauna is a standard in every Finnish house. Men and women have sauna in their own groups, only in a close family circle is the sauna shared together. Its social effect on the Finnish identity is best demonstrated through its open hospitality.

Finnish winter

The time of my departure from Finland arrived. I learned to know Arja up close in her own environment. I was received very openly in a naturally kind atmosphere. I felt very good about this and took this experience, like a precious gift, back home.

We tend to look more often at other people's experiences instead of creating our own. What matters in life are our own experiences. Lots of people deny unwittingly the elements of a romance in their own lives. Romance is the preparation for a lasting happiness. Everything that starts small will succeed.

Back home, reality caught up with me. Money had to be raised for the next university terms. In Finland I had a good time and now was a time for work. The company in my hometown again provided me with employment and badly-needed income. This time the job again exceeded my expectations.

Terror in Germany

Going back to uni became disrupted by a group of intellectually-misled terrorists. The group called Baader-Meinhoff targeted the university of Heidelberg to disrupt its operation and to publicise their disillusionment with today's society. They pursued changes, not through democratic constant processes within a society, but embarked on terror to 'shake the boat' in order to achieve their ideological goals which were incompatible with present realities.

This was the last thing I needed – disruption of my new direction. The head of this plot had been a Gymnasium student from my hometown. He had achieved excellent results. The father of one of my friends was his teacher and had the highest regards for this student. Nobody could ever think that this student, Martin Klar, would emerge as the leader of an extremist group. He misled everybody with his extraordinary intellect. For over two years, the Baader-Meinhoff group successfully disrupted Heidelberg University. At the same time this plot directed fear into ranks of industry bosses and politicians. When the terror taskforces thought they had closed in on Martin Klar, he even managed to engage their helicopter in his escape abroad. What a failure for the police force that had the task to protect the public! For me, this whole debacle had wasted my time. I tried to change to a different university, but the new term had already started, so I had to stick to Heidelberg. The costs of a term against a much-reduced progress in studies became also a consideration. Nobody could predict any outcome of this uproar.

Why do intelligent people embark on terror?

It was not only their input, but also a failure of the society to address education realistically. Extremists do not consider that changes can be gradually achieved with the support of a majority and not enforced by a minority.

I decided to turn my back to Heidelberg University for the time being. Let them sort out their mess and hopefully I could return later.

I also sought the advice of Professor Reinbach, a well respected personality, who was Dean of the medical faculty. He had survived the war despite enduring years of imprisonment. He started his studies at an advanced age but had no formal trade to fall back on. On the other hand, I had the basis of a technical profession that was in demand around the world.

From this perspective, I decided to join a friend and escape for a few weeks into warmer regions. My back problem was very much behind this holiday.

Morocco

Travelling companions

A motorcycle helped us to gain more independence on our trip to Spain. The same friend who had I travelled with to Berlin, Frank, now occupied the back seat of our motorcycle. We banked on BMW's reputation to have a reliable tour of Spain. We took our backpacks, a tent, sleeping bags and one guitar.

We drove quickly through Southern France and did not stop in familiar places. Once we reached Spain we headed to the rugged coastline of Costa Brava. The weather was sunny, but not very warm as it was just early spring. We decided to head further south and find warmer weather.

We stopped at the wharves in the city of Barcelona. When we looked back from there to the city and its mountain ranges behind, we saw a statue of Columbus pointing with his right hand raised towards the Mediterranean telling the world: "The discovery of the 'New World' took place from here."

We were surprised to find towards the city centre a restaurant called Heidelberg. Traffic through this city moved constantly, as one could expect for a place of this size. We had to ask for directions to find our way through Barcelona. It wasn't easy driving through the traffic on a motorbike. We had to stop on the side of the road, take our helmets off, secure the bike and finally approach a person on the footpath. On one occasion, the traffic controller at a main intersection abandoned his centre position through the moving traffic and came towards us. He answered our request for directions by stopping all traffic and indicating to us to continue in the right direction. What a friendly gesture!

Valencia, further south, became the first place we decided to take the plunge into the water of the local beach which was crowded with tourists from all over the world. This was not exactly what we were after because we had to keep an eye on our motorbike and our belongings. Another beach-going attempt in Alicante, again further south, turned out the same way. Our ride through the Sierra Nevada towards Granada presented us with snowfields. In Guadix, we encountered a hamlet of ancient housing called 'cuevas'. Living rooms were carved into the rock walls of a mountain. The home's entrance was marked by a white-painted house front, chimneys pointed to the sky above each stepped rock hill. Children sat on the upper edge of the house wall, which had only one row of tiles. They were sitting on the roof of their house.

These 'cuevas' were spread around the rocky outcrops of the mountain. We were invited to go into one of these cave houses. The lighting was so dim that it took a while to recognise the interior, its few possessions reflected cleanliness with immaculate order.

Such cave housing provided effective insulation against the cold of a winter and the summer heat. The stable temperature of a cave had also its health benefits.

Our next destination was the fabulous city of Granada, a historical place, where different cultures crossed in history including the Arab-Islamic culture which has given this place its distinct image.

Surrounded by high mountain ranges, the Alhambra building is like a fairytale world with a fortress appearance from the outside, but a highly sophisticated art-interior leading to cultivated gardens.

You could spend a whole day looking through this treasure-house with its huge ebony door, column passages, fountains, a lion fountain in a courtyard and richly decorated interiors of Arabic design.

The cathedral in Granada's centre is as splendid as its oriental counterpart – the Alhambra.

Alhambra, Granada, Spain

Alhambra – entrance, Granada

An excursion on foot into the outskirts of Granada brought us face to face with a local guitar maker. A small window allowed a glimpse into the workshop. A bench across a room was loaded with pieces of timber – a few guitar bodies in various stages. As we looked through the window, the master appeared at the door. An elderly man dressed in an apron said: "The master is at work." We replied: "Good morning, senor." He saw our guitar and asked: "Do you play guitar?" We showed our guitar to the master and he asked us to play for him, which we did. The senor disappeared into his workshop and returned with his own guitar and invited us into his house before starting to play. Three glasses with a bottle of red wine found their place on the bench between work pieces. A sip of wine followed by the Spanish salute 'salutas pesetas' encouraged our senor to play his guitar. And how he played, a real master!

We told the master that we had no money to buy a guitar, but this did not worry him. "You are my guests."

It's also worth mentioning that we had a Spanish language guide with us to help our conversation. Language is a vital element in connecting with people of other countries and enhancing our own experiences.

The senor's guitar performance was outstanding – we only could learn from it and realised how much more practice we needed to be anywhere near as good as him. He obviously enjoyed our company and took his time opening another door to show us his master guitars.

On the road, Southern Spain

Street scene, Southern Spain

The guitars hung inside a cupboard with glass doors. The inlaid work on the deck of a guitar distinguishes a Spanish guitar. It is not accidental that this inlaid work shows a design of Arabic origin, because the migration of the guitar points right back to today's Iran.

We could express only our highest admiration to this dedicated Spanish guitar builder. Time during this afternoon passed unnoticed and then we realised it was time to return to the city and our motorcycle. The guitar master insisted that he escorts us back so that we would not get lost. Spanish kindness at its best – taking the time to connect to other people and making the most out of life with Spanish generosity and hospitality.

We headed back from Granada in its high mountain surroundings to the coast towards Malaga. Close to Africa, the climate here was much warmer. Palm trees became a common sight, sugarcane fields surrounded the Malaga plains. A farmer harvested the cane the old way with a large bush knife and gave us a taste of freshly-cut cane. Only young green cane releases the sugar sap when you cut it into small pieces and chew it. Even cultivated banana trees decorated a park. This was the first time

I had seen a banana tree with its distinct downwards hanging dark-purple flower from where the bananas start to develop. Our presence in the park attracted a number of children and they asked us to play the guitar for them. They had a lot of fun with our conversation.

Sugar-cane farmer, Malaga

Here, we were not far from the most southern tip of Europe, opposite Africa. On the way we visited Gibraltar. It was strange to cross a border in Spain with passport control. England claimed this rock peninsula. Surprisingly, the people we met in the narrow streets hugged by steep rock walls spoke Spanish and not English as we had anticipated.

The massive rock formation of Gibraltar shows large sections of its slopes concreted into smooth surfaces. These are to collect rain water. This was their only water supply facility. No wonder there is no official passage, even for climbers to the top ridge, which runs from north to south high up across the peninsula. This did not stop us finding an ascent to the top ridge. The 360 degree panoramic view offered us a look across the Strait of Gibraltar right into Morocco. Big ships pushed their way from the Atlantic Ocean into the Mediterranean Sea in both directions. The weather was perfect, people hardly saw much bad weather here. The view to Africa had a magic influence on our next movement. Being that close to Africa, we decided to set foot across Gibraltar Strait. Our motorcycle with most of our belongings was left at a private address.

Gibraltar rock from its top

A ship took us from Algeciras over to Ceuta on the African continent for a reasonable fare. Ceuta lies opposite Gibraltar, the town stands out as a Spanish territory on African soil. There must have been a barter deal in which England claimed Gibraltar and Spain claimed Ceuta.

Sooner or later this situation must become an apple of discord between England and Spain.

After our arrival on African soil we started hitch-hiking. To our surprise, hitch-hiking worked in Morocco. We soon realised what a different world we had entered when we crossed the border from Ceuta into Morocco. Islam determines here the way of life, people were not dressed the European way. Women were dressed in straight, black costumes from their feet to their head, leaving only the face, and in many cases only the eyes, uncovered. Men could wear what they wanted.

The tribal population of the Berber people were clothed in a wool costume, which also covers the whole body to the feet. A hood was attached to this 'dshelaba' to protect against the sun. Most people were here on foot, traffic was found mainly around cities. Donkeys were used to move everything. Houses in the country were built mostly out of clay bricks dried in the sun.

On our first day in Morocco we reached the city of Rabat on the coast. A lady gave us a lift on the last leg to this city. Her style of dress told us she was not from this country. After a brief French conversation she switched over to German and told us: "I am from Switzerland and work with my husband at the local hospital. Would you like to stay in our house overnight?" She was very eager to talk to us. She must have missed that dialogue in her own language. Her home appeared rather modest and was in a densely-populated area. As visitors in a country of a different culture, we followed our host's advice and did not make our presence noticeable. The husband had night shift at the hospital. A long conversation followed. The lady doctor explained to us how difficult life was for her coming from Switzerland and living in such a different world. As a woman she could do nothing, even as a foreign doctor. "I love my husband. He is also a good doctor, but our life is very limited, because he is a Moroccan. They want western progress here, but not the western way of life. They are bound to their religious traditions of Islam. We have to live in constant caution not to create controversy between our professional task and the established tradition. You don't know how free and easy life is in our countries."

The rest of this night we had a brief sleep in a bed specially prepared for us. We had to leave very early in the morning, so as not to attract unnecessary curiosity in the neighbourhood. After a modest breakfast in this friendly atmosphere, the hostess gave us a lift in her car to the southern outskirts of Rabat. This experience told us how good life was at home.

Our tour continued further south to Marrakech, a traditional trading place on the foothills of the mighty Atlas mountains.

After we were dropped on the side of the road outside Rabat, the sun started to appear on the horizon. The night air was still cold. The heat of the day was yet to come. This was also the time for the 'muezzin' to announce the Koran from the minaret of a mosque. Every Islam believer stops where he is, bows to his knees in the direction of Mecca and pays his respect. This call from a minaret could be heard from far and wide.

The long continuous call filled this quiet, cold morning air.

In front of us, on the same side of the road, a Moroccan man disappeared suddenly into the ditch. Only the call from the minaret indicated to us that this man was doing his duty as a Muslim. We tried to keep a low profile so as not to disturb such religious devotion.

Islam gives its followers a strong order through life – a value not to be underestimated. People with a faith are often spared the search for a purpose in their existence. An individual can eventually answer such a question to our existence, whereas a mass of people will not unanimously find agreement because of their diversity. I believe that it is better for an individual to believe in something that gives his life an order, than believing in nothing and having a deficit in knowledge. Life teaches us – we never come to a final understanding on this 'knowledge highway', which has no limits. Restrictions with modesty give us back in life the quality we are after.

On the outskirts of Rabat, the morning sun had risen on the horizon high above a silhouette of mountain ranges. The cold of the night disappeared quickly. After a couple of hours we were still waiting on the side of the road for a car to give us a lift. The traffic was anything but busy this morning, so we had to prepare ourselves for a long wait. I took out my guitar to make time go faster. Soon after a black limousine stopped. A female person got out of the car and raised her arm, indicating us to come closer. As we moved into this direction, the car reversed towards us. This lady helped us store our backpacks away into the back of the car and told us confidentially: "I told the driver you are our friends". In the limousine there was a young man on the back seat. We all found room on that seat. The driver continued southwards towards Casablanca. My guitar came with me. We introduced each other as the car drove at high speed.

Chris and her companion came from America's West. They were touring like us, but could afford to hire this car because of their strong American dollar.

While we rushed towards Casablanca, our guitar and songs transformed the limousine into a 'musical theatre'. Our driver was obviously delighted with the music from the back of his car. The young lady, Chris, surprised us when she took the guitar and gave an excellent performance of Bach. Still waters always run deep!

When we reached Casablanca, we decided to stick together and look for affordable accommodation. The most common language for foreigners to communicate in Morocco was French – a relic of colonial times. Our American counterparts could not speak much French, so we helped out with pleasure.

We decided to go shopping for food. On our way to a shopping centre, we were talking so much that we overlooked traffic on a pedestrian crossing. Only a quick reaction saved our companion Chris from being run over by a car.

After this incident, we found accommodation in a youth hostel. A cultural problem surfaced here. Chris was supposed to stay with the local women separately in another part of the building.

A brief in-house consultation resulted that Chris could stay with us. A decision not entirely welcomed by other occupants of the room. We thought it was safer that Chris stay with us than with a 'harem' of Moroccan women. She was dressed too much in a western style for that.

The cooler air outside in a park with its benches invited us to enjoy an improvised dinner: bread, cheese, chocolate, milk and oranges. Our two American companions travelled quite luxuriously by the looks of their modern suitcases compared with our backpacks. Chris moved closer to us to find out how we had prepared our dinner using our boy-scout expertise.

The night in the youth hostel passed quietly until the early morning hours when one of the Moroccan occupants made indecent moves on Chris. She was sleeping between us in my army sleeping bag. We then decided to get up and leave the room all together. Chris, as a blond, good looking young woman, awoke the emotions of Moroccan men. We were lucky that this incident did not have further consequences for us.

After a boy-scout breakfast, our American friends caught the bus to Marrakech. We wanted to give hitch-hiking a try again to save money. We agreed to meet up again in Marrakech. Only a few lifts enabled us to reach our destination on the same day.

Against the background of the Atlas mountain range with eternal snow on its peaks, Marrakech gave an imposing impression with the all-dominant mosque and its tall minaret. Alleys started from a central place with colourful Arab characters such as the waterman carrying shiny brass bowls and the butcher busy behind his desk in the open trying to keep the flies off his exhibits. Wooldye works were displayed high up the alleys in intensive colour patterns.

Water-seller, Marrakech

Wool-dye works, Marrakech

Touring team, 1966, Morocco

Raising your eyes from the markets, you see brown mountain slopes climbing into light, misty clouds. With a second look you could make out a white band of snow continuing into the sky. Down here in the city it was extremely hot, up there reigned winter!

No other tourists were around so it was easy to find our American friends. Once we found each other in the main market place, we sat down in an open Arab café and ordered a cup of strong, sweet black tea. For the remaining daylight hours, I talked to Chris about my life. She just listened. I had never before told anybody such details about my life. All she brought forward was: "I come from a small farming village called Connell in the State of Washington and just have finished my university studies touring mainly Europe with a friend." While we talked, my friend talked to Chris' friend David. They were engulfed in scientific discussions as David had just finished his studies in physics.

It was here in Marrakech where a friendship started to grow out of this accidental meeting. This friendship is still current and well alive some 40 years later. Even long periods of time apart did not spoil this friendship. Maintaining a friendship through a lifetime is one of life's greatest assets. Most people change during the course of their life living more and more distanced from their past. How many friends have we left from our 'journey of a lifetime'? Very few, if any, we can call a real friend!

That night, we found a cheap accommodation in separate places not far from our meeting place. The call from the minaret penetrated the silence just before the sun announced a new day on the horizon. In the alleys footsteps could be heard, a car engine started, wheels from a donkey cart bumped through the holes in the road.

We got up early and caught the bus into the mountains, where the Sahara desert begins. Our destination was Ouarzazate, an oasis on a plateau behind the Atlas mountain ranges. Our friends didn't join us, they wanted to go to the beach which was still a fair distance away from Marrakech. I reminded Chris: "We are in a Muslim country! Women don't go here to the beach like we do." We found out, on our return that they had followed this advice.

Before we caught the bus to Ouarzazate, we bought a 'dshelaba' – a dress of the local Berbers woven out of fine goat wool. It helped us also to mix better into the local population so that we could not readily be identified as foreigners. Another advantage of this costume was that all our trouser pockets were hidden, so we were less likely to lose anything. It seemed strange to us to wear a complete wool cover during this heat of the day, but the outfit served in a very efficient way by regulating the temperature against the heat of the day and cold of the night.

During our bus trip, we saw hamlets with houses in a rising valley. The houses were built from clay blocks and did not have any windows. The brown colour of these houses blended in so well with the landscape – they were almost invisible. Next to the settlements, terraces were built out of the same materials and were planted with barley and some vegetables. The bright green of these terraces stood out against the settlements. Water here was very carefully managed, nothing was wasted. The water was directed through small channels within the terraces to drip-irrigate from the top. This was done only at night. A reservoir caught the excess water which was carried by women in clay jugs every night to the top channel of the terraces. It is a harsh life in this mountain desert environment. People depend entirely on their barley crops and their livestock of goats. Nothing else could be cultivated here.

Hamlet, Atlas mountains

The bus travelled a dirt road all day, stopping on request from people on the bus or on the road. We were the only foreigners on the bus, but blended in quite well with our Moroccan outfits. When people came closer to us, they found out, with a smile, that we were not one of them.

We arrived in the oasis of Ouarzazate before dusk. A main road connected low block houses on both sides and these were painted in many different colours. Trees along a footpath gave the impression of a lively town.

Not far from this road, we saw a rock wall, which was the boundary of the oasis and protected the settlement against the endless sands of Sahara desert.

A dirt road circled the oasis near that wall and connected on either side to the main road. A well-established orange orchard could be found there as well – dark orange shined through its green foliage. A Moroccan boy held oranges for sale in a woven basket along the main road. We never had oranges of that size in our hands. They looked so perfect and tasted intensively like their skin does. Late afternoon we observed some slim-built, tall, barefoot women carrying full jugs of water on their heads with only one hand securing the jug. Each tree in the orchard was watered from a well in the town centre. The sun sets quickly in the Sahara so only a limited time was available for these chores. Carrying water was one task in the oasis and a number of women were dedicated to it – there was no escape from this strict organisation.

Ourarzazate-oasis, Morocco

Silence was the dominant feature in the oasis, broken only by the call from the minaret and the occasional 'hee-haw' of a donkey. Everybody lived here in peace and quiet. They were happy and you could read content in their faces. This was the first time we had watched life in an oasis and it was an exceptional experience.

We spent the first night in a modest private accommodation. The next day we went outside the oasis. Behind the oasis wall was a river without water – a wadi. In times of heavy rainfall, which occurs very rarely, the wadi can carry masses of water in its river bed. The oasis wall protects against nature's fury. In the dry season, the wadi looks like a desert road. On the other side of the wadi there was a well-protected brilliant green field of barley. We set our foot towards this field to have a closer look at what a woman was doing in the middle of the field.

She was constantly bending down and picking something off the ground; what, we did not know. Upon closer inspection, we realised that she was weeding the field without causing damage to the crop. All the barley must have been planted by exact measurement as all the stalks were of the same height. They looked healthy like everything else in this desert that receives the gift of water.

'Special attention' is the motto for people living in the desert – there is no room for 'experiments'. Such natural restrictions guarantee people's survival. They seem to be happy, because they don't know much else. As soon as such conditions are subjected to change, everything else will change. The desert, an advanced eco-system, can teach us to support limited human activity. Only tough people manage to make a living in a desert. They should teach us this survival process.

In upcoming years I had other opportunities to build on my experiences in a desert environment. This time we had to be content with a two-day visit to the Ouarzazate oasis. The bus returned us in the morning of the third day to Marrakech. We were not sure whether our American friends were still around. They would not recognise us in our Berber dresses. But soon after we arrived, Chris found us. She was watching the people leaving the bus and, when it came to our turn, we were welcomed with a big hello. Somebody must have studied the bus timetable.

For the rest of the day we gathered in the centrally-located café with our American friends exchanging our experiences of the last couple of days.

From the café, which was on an elevated platform of timber planks, we could watch the busy life around us for hours. A water truck also arrived spraying water on to the dust. The air became immediately fresh again. Life unfolded around us – men, women in Moroccan dresses, an occasional businessman in a western-style suit passed by. Small trucks, that looked home-made and carriages pulled by a man or donkey, also made their way through this central place.

Our meeting with the American couple was our last as we had to return home. We exchanged addresses and bid farewell. Unforeseen circumstances with unexpected people in a foreign place create strong memories in all of us.

A friendship is true through life, when destiny finds ways to reconnect. Chris was in my good books.

Before going home, I said to our American friends: "Our understanding of life on a beach is not the same in a Muslim country. A woman in a bikini is taking unacceptable risks in such a country. We have to accept different cultures and their different sensitivities. People are not all the same."

Our hitch-hiking through Morocco back to the ferry to take us over the Strait of Gibraltar went surprisingly fast and without incident. Crossing the Strait was very interesting. Dolphins swam with the ship as if they enjoyed the race. Just before our arrival in Algeciras we passed the giant rocks of the Gibraltar peninsula.

Back on European soil, we went to the house where our motorbike was being stored by a Spanish family. It was still there, exactly as we had left it. We showed our appreciation by presenting them with a souvenir from Morocco.

I had to be back in Heidelberg for certain terms at the university and hoped the terrorist interruptions had ceased allowing normal studies to continue.

No time was left for further sightseeing. A stop at Punta de Tarifa gave us the opportunity to say goodbye to Africa. The Atlas mountains greeted us from a far distance across the wild ocean movement of the Atlantic.

It was still a long way home which we had to cover in as little as two days to keep our timetable. We were two on our motorbike, but with only one licensed driver. It would have been nice if we could have swapped the driver's seat from time to time. To try this, we stopped in a small village on the way to Sevilla. I tried my best to teach my friend how to ride a motorbike. During this exercise, some locals watched our training with curiosity. When it came to my friend's first attempt to ride the motorbike, these onlookers were rewarded with a spectacle. My friend let the machine go too fast, bike and driver got separated from one another, both ending up on the road. No more trials, my friend's confidence had reached an absolute low. My friend now needed a cushion so that he could reclaim the back seat of the bike.

The long hours of driving were difficult for both of us. The driver of a motorbike has the bonus of constant fresh air to stay alert. This is very different to a car driver. Can somebody drive a car non-stop 3000km from Algeciras to Heidelberg? My passenger developed a strategy to cope with the long hours of driving, looking for half an hour to the left, half an hour straight and half an hour to the right.

The engine wanted to go on strike just before Sevilla when we were travelling at 180 km per hour. Only quick action with the clutch prevented the engine from seizing. My friend was hanging on to my neck. I knew we could not travel at 180 km per hour anymore, keeping the speed at under 100km per hour. Our engine recovered with new oil. This way we succeeded in getting back home with no more trouble.

A lunch break in Sevilla in front of the marvellous cathedral became our only rest. Cordoba would have been nice to explore, but it had to be left for another time. We travelled for hours through highlands with extensively-cultivated olive groves on our way to Madrid, the capital of Spain. At this time of the year, in the spring, Spain is green and blossoming. Seasonal rain transforms this country for a short period from summer dryness into a garden of Eden. This area before Madrid is called Estremadura. The wet, dark soil around millions of olive trees was thoroughly ploughed. The light silvery green of their leaves gave the area a fresh appearance. Grasslands in between were covered with colourful spring flowers. As a contrast, there were mountains with snow caps on the horizon – Sistema Central and its Sierra Guadarrama. In Madrid we left behind its big Avenidas, Palacio Central, magnificent buildings and gardens to continue our trip home. Towards Zaragoza the weather got colder. Our motorbike welcomed these conditions as it didn't run hot anymore.

Barcelona, Southern France, the German border near Freiburg – we nearly made it. But we arrived on a Sunday afternoon and it took hours to get through border control, because of long queues of weekend holidaymakers. Such an introduction into our own country was definitely not part of our plan. After this delay, we had to stop for a rest before beginning the last leg of our journey. A good, long sleep was on our minds – nothing else.

This latest tour had distracted me from the realities of life at Heidelberg University. Nobody could do anything. Protests at the university reached new levels when armed conflict took place. I could not afford to watch this kind of conflict any longer, so I returned to the job in my hometown where I could live undisturbed and save money for my future. During this time I received a letter from Chris, whom I had met in Morocco. She wrote from Paris. I wanted to see her again before she returned to America. She indicated she would be in London with family friends at the end of June. I wanted to find out whether it was possible to find work in the north-west of the United States.

An international employment agency in Frankfurt got me in contact with Boeing in Seattle. The offer was too good to refuse. A manager from Seattle came to Frankfurt to see me, but an event of far-reaching consequences stopped me thinking about this direction. A school mate, who had only recently migrated to America, was killed in action in Vietnam.

London

I could spare a few days to go to London to see Chris in June close to my 25th birthday. Initially my motorbike left me high and dry on the way on the Autobahn to Holland. The engine lost oil again. I had to stop and return slowly back to Heidelberg.

This didn't mean the end of my plans to see Chris in London. I hitch-hiked to London. With luck on my side, I arrived in London not much later than I would have with my own transport. I arrived on a Friday, right on time to be at Chris' address outside London on the weekend. England showed its best with warm and sunny weather. For the remainder of this first day in London I enjoyed some of the many sights London could offer. I took accommodation for the night in a youth hostel. The next morning, as I had limited time, I left the city centre. At Trafalgar Square, a huge number of wooden stairs took me down to the underground station. I tried to get a ticket upstairs. The exchange in coins confused me. I didn't know if the amount was correct. I held in my hand a sixpence, three pence, shillings and other coins. What I did not realise was that I had been noticed by criminals who followed me unobserved. When the train arrived, I was just stepping through the doors, when a man suddenly pushed me hard from the side into the carriage and I fell to the floor. Another man forced my wallet out of my pocket before I could get up. The automated doors started to close and the two men ran off the train. Physically I was all right, but I knew I now had a problem. I reported this incident to the staff at the next station. There was little chance of seeing my wallet again. What should I do when I was so close to the address I wanted to visit? I decided to go ahead with the planned visit. Only after the incident did I remember having seen the two men next to me when I purchased my ticket. They must have realised I was a foreigner and followed me into the tube. They were certainly professional crooks. At the second station I was handed a new return ticket so I could continue my trip. The youth hostel near my destination was sympathetic to my situation and gave me two nights accommodation free of charge. During that first night at the youth hostel, I met a number of very interesting people who came from different parts of the world. Social, philosophical and down-to-earth discussions were held. I met very open-minded people, open to the world.

On Sunday I went to Chris' address. The weather was still warm and sunny as it should be in the summer. A park around a lake attracted many locals. I joined in this peaceful atmosphere and rested on a perfect English lawn enjoying the warmth of the sun. I started to think about how to introduce myself at the home where Chris was staying. I felt quite nervous. Some locals helped me with directions to the address. When they heard about my mishap with the underground in London, the brother of a lady, who ran the local taxi business offered me a lift to the address I was looking for. He knew I had no money, but he still invited me to join him. During this short drive he revealed that his brother played soccer in Germany and I wished his brother success. The taxi stopped in front of a fairly-new, two-storey house with a small garden. I thanked the driver who offered me his business card and a lift back, when required.

I rang the bell at the house and waited. After a while, two window shutters opened under the gables. Chris welcomed me waving her hands. A few moments later the entrance door of the house opened and the whole family invited me to come in. Chris rushed down the stairs inside the house from the attic. Despite the fact that the people didn't know me, I received a very warm welcome. Chris had her long blond hair cut short which gave me a surprise. But isn't this what women like? To surprise you? Chris looked somehow younger. My introduction was not necessary as it seemed everybody was informed about me.

The decision to send me and Chris for a walk outside was taken unanimously. We had a lot to catch up on since we had left Marrakech. We sat on a bench along a walkway which overlooked a small village. I did not mention anything to Chris about my incident in the underground. I should have told her, so she would have understood why I had to go back to London the next day. Happy people don't count hours. It was mainly me who did the talking. Chris was listening. We never asked one another how old we were. I had a feeling we must have been about the same age. Chris had finished her education as an art teacher in America and she liked to travel as I did.

Her family was running a wheat farm in the north-west of the United States. After her studies, Chris had worked one year in Seattle to raise funds for her European tour. We also spoke about issues concerning our future. When the cold of the night arrived with the sunset, we returned to the house. The house was all ours, everybody else had gone out. Chris prepared a quick sandwich, which I welcomed because I was really hungry. When Chris went upstairs, I checked my watch and was surprised to see that it was 11pm. My first thoughts went to the youth hostel. I did not know how I could get back there in the middle of the night. When Chris was halfway down the stairs, I told her I had to leave immediately for the hostel. Chris didn't say anything. She directed me to the back door of the house. What did she mean with that, didn't she want me to leave at all?

A 'switch' for our destiny was turned off here. Had we misunderstood each other through a lack of communication from both sides? Not even a romantic farewell could change our situation. I do care about this friendship and that is why I re-live our friendship through these words.

I'd like to remind critics of my representation that most people read or talk about other people's lives with their struggles, success, disappointments and romance. They never come to an account of it in their own life. They are too busy upholding an image to be in line with everybody else. Civil courage is also a true reflection of one's own life.

Everybody remembers a first kiss. The appreciation of this friendship remained through all our lives, despite misunderstandings and long disruptions through time and distance. A friendship lasting through a lifetime is a treasure in everybody's life.

During the short time we met, we realised that we had a broad spectrum of interests. We had affection for one another, but something did not want to work out for us at that time.

Was this because we were too similar in many regards? Same polarities repel, only different polarities attract? Was Chris waiting for me to make an overture? Was I hesitating in our friendship because I was not clever enough to reach Chris' intellectual level?

Anyway, when I left Chris that night I found myself back in an unwanted reality. A car stopped on the side of the road and the driver asked me: "Where are you heading?" I entered the car but got out again as soon as possible because the driver had other things on his mind. When I finally arrived on foot at the hostel, the gate in the stone wall was locked. Nobody could be seen in the building. I was determined not to spend the rest of this night in front of this gate. I climbed the wall and managed to come down unnoticed. The door to the dormitory remained open, so I gained access to the folding bed, where my backpack waited. It took only a few moments to fall asleep.

The next morning, when life in the youth hostel started, I got up and moved outside. I wanted to avoid questions from the supervisor as to how I had entered the hostel late last night. But everybody was under the impression that I just had returned to the hostel.

Today was Monday. I had to go to London to organise my return with the German Embassy. I was a bit confused. Should I have told Chris why I had to leave? She most certainly must have taken my departure personally – as if I did not like her. I should have made an effort to call her on the phone at least, but I had no money, so I had to leave for London.

At the German Embassy I received the initial welcome: "Another globe-trotter". They had heard stories of stolen wallets before and were not very sympathetic. Their attitude changed only when I demanded to see the Consul-General. Eventually, I received the boat passage over the Channel and a train ticket for the remaining distance home. I understood quite well that I had to reimburse the borrowed money.

The initial treatment I received at the Embassy made me wonder just how well our own citizens are regarded abroad. As I learned later, from contact with other embassies, our own citizens didn't always receive the attention they deserved. Once I had to make an enquiry in South Africa at the German Embassy and received this response: "We will only take somebody out of the country in a coffin". They did not understand my enquiry, at first. Perhaps they were dealing with a strange case just before I turned up? But this wouldn't justify such inconsistent behaviour. On another occasion in Caracas/Venezuela, I and my family received a similarly strange reception at the German Embassy.

Are the German Embassy staff under stress abroad? A customer complaint system could help here. But it is common knowledge that when you complain, it is likely nobody listens.

Arja – first Germany visit

Back in Heidelberg I had to decide whether to continue with part of my studies that were not affected by the turmoil at Heidelberg University or to follow-up the offer from Boeing in America.

The raging war in Vietnam became a deterrent in my decision to move to America.

My decision was supported by a surprise visit from Arja in Finland. What a surprise! Will I be the 'cock of the walk' between Arja from Finland and Chris from America?

This was an unexpected experience for me, so I decided to keep my head cool and be friendly to both girls for the time being.

On one day of her visit, Arja accompanied me to Frankfurt where I cancelled my application with Boeing. The weather was miserable on that day, barely 10 degrees and drizzle – and this was during a German summer. Fortunately we also had sunny days during her visit and I was happy to return the hospitality that she and her family had shown me in Finland.

Heidelberg had many worthwhile sightseeing places with its historic narrow city centre, the river Neckar with its bridges, wooded hills on both sides leading into the plains of the river Rhine. The castle overlooks the entire city from castle hill, which accommodates the largest wooden wine barrel in the world – its rulers must have loved their wine!

I also showed Arja the university and all its faculties which were spread around the historical city centre. I introduced her to my friends and on these occasions she remained very silent, showing her guarded Scandinavian nature.

We were more reserved than the youth of today but were looking at the bright side of life. I had a girlfriend who was only separated by distance and time. If you expect me to write about intimate relations, I have to disappoint you, because no matter in what time we are living, a good friendship has to build on independence first. Then only develops a lasting commitment which is the basis for a close relationship.

In those days there was much less entertainment for young people. Outside influences did not interfere with traditional efforts at home, school and work. I must admit we were, to a certain degree, more slowly developed in life and most probably a bit naïve. I also acknowledge that each generation lives its life with peculiarities that are characteristic of its time. There are fluctuations from generation to generation and everything around us is on a move. We cannot stop this from happening, but we can grab hold of the positive sides of life even though the negatives are still there. Time can help us learn, how to distance the negative inputs in our life.

Arja left again for Finland as a good friend with a renewed commitment to keep our friendship alive.

As I had called off the engagement with Boeing in America, I decided to stay in Heidelberg and work out how I could continue my studies despite the disruption at the university. What had other students done? They had either lost time, changed university or did something else.

At that time, I was staying with a teacher's family in Eppelheim, a suburb of Heidelberg. A friend of mine, a talented artist, came to see me. He wanted to work for a short time in Heidelberg and needed accommodation. I put in a good word for him with the landlord to allow him to share my room for a few nights while he looked for his own accommodation.

But this arrangement did not last long. My friend, whose name was also Martin, soon had to leave after breaking house rules – and I had to go with him!

I spent my days at university while my friend followed his artistic inspiration – often returning late at night by climbing the ladder from the house wall to reach our room in the attic.

We were lucky that all this had escaped the landlord's attention. But one Sunday morning my friend decided to have a good wash from the garden tap and stripped all his clothes off. The landlady caught a glimpse of this action and yelled through her window: "This is going too far!" She hurried to our attic and demanded entrance:

"Mister Martin, this is the end, you have to leave with your friend immediately. What are people around here thinking of us?"

Despite this unfortunate incident, I stuck with my friend. We packed up and moved out rather than try to pacify a landlord whose reputation relied entirely on the people in the neighbourhood – especially being a local school teacher.

Artist Martin had to look after himself from now on, whereas I had to find my own way. But luck was on my side. I visited a friend who, by chance, was about to move to England on a one-year student exchange. His landlady knew me and had no objection that I took over his room. I found myself back 'on dry land'.

Life at the university continued mainly in the new teaching departments outside the city. The disputes with the Baader-Meinhoff terror organisation remained active in the university's city headquarters.

Life in this city was very different at that time. Because of the Vietnam War, a large number of American military personnel was stationed in Heidelberg. One night when I walked home from an institute with other colleagues, a Volkswagen beetle passed us. Its passengers had nothing better to do than to throw beer bottles at us. Luckily we escaped from any injury. This was, however, not the end of it. My group included the German shotput champion and discus champion. Both of these men over two metres tall weighed at least 130kg each. The two American soldiers received a lesson they will never forget.

After the bottles were thrown, we all turned towards the car, grabbed the bumper bar at the back and lifted the back wheels off the road so that the car could not move. When one of the passengers dared to turn against us, our shotput champion grabbed the soldier by his neck and his leg and threw him out of the car on to the road.

A second soldier received a similar treatment. What was a joyride for these soldiers had now ended up with them passed out on the road. We called the police from a nearby telephone box. The military police arrived on the scene and the two drunken, unconscious soldiers disappeared in the back of the police van. This was not an isolated incident in Heidelberg at that time. The training camp for missions in Vietnam created a dangerous climate for the civilian population of this city. Attempts were made by the American administration to curb the violence. The American military even bought a whole wrecking yard of cars. At this yard they supplied their soldiers with sledge hammers which they used to smash the cars to get rid of their unwanted tension build-up. Eventually, after the Vietnam war, peace returned to the streets of Heidelberg.

I wouldn't be surprised that a lot of people have lost memories of this time. We are often better losing some memories.

Amsterdam

During that year I received a letter from Chris. She did not write from England, but gave me the address of the American Express in Amsterdam and asked me to write her at this address. Instead of writing I decided to go to Amsterdam and, with a bit of luck, I got there within one day by hitch-hiking. The American Express couldn't give me an address for Chris. I decided to leave a letter for her. It was a long letter that said all I wanted to tell her.

The next morning I turned up again at the American Express and I continued to do so for another 10 days. There was no note, no sign of Chris. My patience started to wear very thin so I 'bit the bullet' and returned to Heidelberg. I could not afford to lose more study time.

Two weeks later I received a letter from Chris from Amsterdam saying that she was soon returning to America. She suggested we meet again. There was no mention of my letter. Was it possible that she did not receive it at all? My affection for Chris turned into rejection; the elements of affection and rejection are very closely intertwined.

I wrote a note back to the Amsterdam address wishing Chris a good return voyage to America.

Silence entered our friendship. Neither of us knew any more what really was going on. It took decades for light to return to our friendship. Our sympathy for one another did not get lost. Almost 40 years later, life gave us the opportunity to re-establish a friendship – a more mature one – that could last for the rest of our lives.

My meeting Chris opened a chapter in both of our lives. I had to make tough decisions and deal with controversy: what I wanted to do versus what I had to do. This is a common conflict in people's lives. As my 'flame' for Chris did not die over 40 silent years, there is reason to be happy with the outcome of our new friendship.

The relationships we build are the real assets in our life. Family relationships are given assets – they are not necessarily what we best identify ourselves with.

We never can know everything in our lives so we must be content with what we know.

Meanwhile, life had to continue for me in Heidelberg. I studied hard to succeed in two consecutive terms at the uni. My accommodation turned out to be quite good. I helped the retired landlady during winter by carrying coal briquettes every morning from the cellar into the house. She was quite happy as long as her tenant did not receive visits from young ladies. This was a very common rule at that time. During the week I enjoyed at least one hot meal a day at the university canteen. I did not cook at my place. There was little time and I am definitely no cook. My dinners usually consisted of porridge, bread and butter, ham, fruit and vegetables. The most I managed to get off a stove was a cup of tea or boiled eggs. That's a student life – time for studies and for very little else!

Through a friend I gained access to a weekly musical event on Friday nights. Chansons and ballads became popular in student circles in 1966/1967. I joined a student club and performed my guitar on a regular basis with songs like Spiel nicht mit den Schmuddle Kindern

(Don't play with those street kids) and George Brassens' Les funerailes d'antan (Earlier funerals) and Les Lilas (The lilies).

I enjoyed the response from the audience. Substantial money could be earned on these occasions to support my life as a student.

For the rest of the year 1966 I did not hear anything from Chris in America, silence between us continued. On the other hand I received the occasional letter from Arja in Finland. She maintained a constant pen-friendship. At one stage, though, I could not understand our relationship any more. This was when Arja sent me a Finnish record wrapped in a magazine without any note. I was very surprised and replied: "Why don't you write any more, have we got nothing to say to each other?" She had a change of heart and started to write again. She admitted much later that she had thought: "The poor bloke, I don't want him to suffer."

During winter 1966/1967 I decided to sell my motorbike. I did not want the expenses with it. The oil-leak on the right cylinder cover had to be fixed before I could sell it. I could not afford to pay a mechanic to fix it, so I asked a nearby motor mechanic if he would allow me to do the repairs in his workshop. The mechanic looked at me and after some hesitation he agreed, with conditions. On two Saturdays I took the motor completely apart to fix the housing. The centre bolt was stripped on one side between the two cylinders. I had to machine a new bore, press a new sleeve in made from the same material and secure the new bolt with a proper cross dowel.

On the second Saturday I assembled the motor and fitted everything back into the frame. The big moment had arrived, would the engine start again?

The mechanic and his staff watched. The engine started with the turn of the key and kept running smoothly. The mechanic shook my hand. "Well done," he said. I was really proud of this achievement as I never had before touched a motorbike.

Now I could sell my motorbike, so I took it to a motorbike shop opposite the university in Karlsruhe. The owner agreed to take my motorbike for a price that was not much less than I had paid. I was also told: "There are plenty of Americans around here who buy a motorbike to travel in Europe." I banked the cheque straight away as I did not want it to be dishonoured.

Towards the end of winter 1966/1967, I received a card from Chris. She had painted a picture on the card featuring cherry branches in blossom. The words on the card were confusing: "I am very happy because I am expecting." No word about the 'other party'. I wondered why I was receiving this information out of the blue. I replied: "Congratulations, I do hope there is a father to look after both of you." I was certainly not the father as I was not sexually progressive enough at that time to put myself in such a position. When I later wrote a brief note asking how her life was going, she replied saying that she was alive and helping her husband in his business. 'We rest how we prepare our bed'.

I was not in a position to effectively help a distant friend as I had enough worries in my own life.

Two semesters at Heidelberg University must have been enough to get the riots started again. As a result, the university was closed indefinitely. At that time my friend came back from England so I had to find other accommodation. The uncertainties at the university made me unsure as what to do next. I also met two of my classmates from the secondary night school in Heidelberg. One of them had changed his studies from physics to medicine hoping for better future prospects.

He was equally upset about the lack of progress at the university. The other student stopped his studies completely and went back to the airforce where he found the recognition he did not have in the university environment despite achieving all first-class marks in his studies.

The more mature a person is with age, the more critical he becomes. Intellectual people do not accept things as they are – they keep asking questions.

In society there are two types of intelligence – theory and practice. In the workforce there are men and women who have a universal intellect by employing theory and practice. There are others who claim intelligence but only have a theoretical intelligence through a formal education. Our education system does not support practice intelligence enough.

A good example of a realistic education is that of a good friend of mine. Like me, he did full training in a technical trade before his studies. His father, a high-profile doctor engineer, supported his son's efforts saying: "Before any studies, learn first what you want to study."

Around the Mediterranean

As university study was at a standstill, a friend and I decided to travel. We read an article about a newspaperman who had just finished a bicycle tour around the Mediterranean. He gave us an inspiration to follow his example, but not on a bicycle as we did not have the time. We were looking for a challenge and so decided to build a car out of two car wrecks. The interior of the VW bus was fitted with benches along the sides and a table in the centre which could be dropped down to form a platform. We fitted curtains along the windows and timber panelling on the walls to make it cosy. Many parts from the wrecks were overhauled and taken on board for spares.

The day of our departure arrived. The cold of winter was still around in March 1967. This tour would be a challenge because we had minimum resources.

I wrote a card to Arja and Chris informing them on the challenge lying ahead of us. I also said this would have been even more of an adventure if they could have participated. (But I knew this was not possible). I gave them both the option to write back to the address of the German Embassy in Cairo/Egypt.

Austria – Yugoslavia – Bulgaria

In the Alps of Austria there was still heavy snow. We could only make it through the Wurzen pass when we unloaded our car at the beginning of the ascent. One of us had to push the car all the way up the 26-degree incline of the road. Once our car reached the top, we went back on foot to collect our belongings. This was an exhausting exercise, but after that the tour continued easily through former Yugoslavia on an Autobahn. We passed the two major cities of Zagreb and Belgrade.

We did not pay special attention to this initial part of our tour as a lot more laid in front of us. On the Bulgarian border visas were required. This was a slow process as we could not speak their language. Over the border we found ourselves in high mountainous country where the cold of the night caught up with us. Early the next morning we drove into Sofia, the capital of Bulgaria. The cold and rainy weather gave us a poor impression of this city. Only the city centre showed some pomp with colossal buildings in the only open space. The grey of the buildings matched the sky of the day. A number of huge statues filled spaces in the wide road of the city centre. No people could be seen, only the occasional agricultural truck bumped across the stone pavement. This atmosphere might change during festival times, we thought.

On the city outskirts, the neglected roads and houses began again. It was here the people lived and we realised the failure of the communist system. As soon as we found ourselves back in the countryside, well-established vineyards restored the natural image of this country.

Turkey

When we reached the border to Turkey, we were glad to leave the bad roads behind us. We faced another lengthy border control process and the customs officials were not pleased about our short visit in Bulgaria.

They insisted that we register our transistor radio in our passports so that we take it out of the country again.

The weather was sunny again and after a short drive we reached the outskirts of Istanbul. The city was pulsing with traffic and people. A constant chaos welcomed us. The door to the Orient opens here. There are no dull, uniform houses lining the roads here. Here the houses' style, colour and appearance reflected the individual abilities of its citizens. People on foot in the streets dressed in European style, Arabic style or any style. They carried textiles, vegetables and pottery. Cafés along the footpaths offered a break from these lively activities. Mainly locals were sitting at small round tables with a cup of tea or coffee in front of them. Some smoked a water-pipe and watched the restless life pass by. All makes of cars were on the road – some veteran cars you wouldn't see elsewhere. Donkeys mixed patiently into this scenery.

As we continued driving, we reached the Straits of Bosporus. On its European side is the mosque Hagia Sofia, a famous Islamic temple. Its rounded dome rose with the minaret tower far above the surrounding houses. Istanbul has a foothold on the European side was as well as the Asian side. Galata Bridge over the Straits of Bosporus joins both parts of the city. Under the bridge, on the Asian side were floating restaurants serving fresh fish. We spent a few hours on the Bosporus waters in a 'cool, calm' restaurant under the bridge. The light movements of the restaurants on the water gave the impression of a moving ship. The fish we consumed was served with a rich variety of vegetables – everything was well prepared and tasted excellent.

Galata bridge, Istanbul

As we came from different conditions in Middle Europe, we were careful to keep a close eye on hygiene to ensure our wellbeing. We met very friendly people – the fact that we hardly spoke their language did not matter.

A phrase book helped us to initiate contact with other people. They would usually respond with a smile and then we would try to communicate in our own language.

Before we continued our tour into the interior of Turkey, we wanted to say hello to a former class mate, Gabi, who was married to a Turkish man and lived in Istanbul. When we arrived at the address, we found ourselves in a suburb of Istanbul where obviously rich people lived. The house was surrounded like all the others with a high stone wall. A steel gate at the entrance allowed only a glimpse into the interior of the property. Stairs leading upwards over a number of garden terraces prevented a view to the house. There was an intercom at the side of the gate for visitors to announce themselves. When somebody answered our intercom call, we briefly introduced ourselves and asked after Gabi.

The intercom connection was all of a sudden disrupted. We heard steps coming down the stairs. The Turkish man had a gun on his side. First we had no explanation for such a demonstration. Then the man, in clear German, asked us to leave. We took off without any further questions. Only later, when we arrived home, did we learn that Gabi had attempted to escape from there and was now kept as a prisoner by her jealous husband. Here was an unfortunate side of a relationship between two very different cultures.

Her husband had studied and lived in Germany for many years. His family was very rich and he spoke fluent German. Yet he maintained his cultural bonds in his home environment. Gabi eventually escaped in a dramatic way, changed her name and lived an incognito life under police protection.

But that day in Istanbul, nothing was holding us back. We immediately continued with our trip to Ankara passing through mountain areas with heavy snow – a black forest scene changed into an alpine mountain scene.

The currency of the country allowed us to stop in a small village along the road and have a low-priced lunch in a restaurant. The news of a foreign presence circulated here in no time. A number of people joined us at our table and tried to have some conversation with us. Despite the language barrier, we were very well served. The restaurant had its small tables lined up in a row against one wall. The entrance of the restaurant was kept wide open to the road so that people could watch the scene on the road from inside. After lunch, the shoe cleaner was waiting for us with his box in front of the restaurant. There was no escape! We had to rest one foot at a time on his stepped box and our shoes received a quick clean with a brush, shoe cream applied with a soft sponge and finally a rolled-up cloth went in a haste over each shoe. We could not recognise our shoes any more – they had never shined like this before. We paid the shoe cleaner a bonus and in no time found ourselves surrounded by other men offering us all sorts of merchandise from trousers and socks to watches. We sought refuge in our car and, making sure no merchandise had been passed into the car, we continued our trip.

Back on the road, the majority of the traffic was trucks. In the middle of the night we passed Ankara, the capital of the country.

From our short visit we could not get much of an impression of the city except that its wide roads with big house blocks made for a bigger city. In its centre stood the statue of Ata Turk, the father of this nation who liberalised its people to a large degree from outdated customs. Turkey was, for that reason, the only Islamic nation where, for instance, women were not allowed to cover their faces.

Our road to the south took us through highlands with barely any vegetation. We stopped at Tuz Golu, a vast salt lake. On its retreated shores we watched a sea eagle circling in the air above the water. This was the first time we had seen an eagle in nature.

We tried to take a photo of the eagle but it proved a challenge – like many wildlife photos.

Travelling on these roads was difficult because of the amount of truck traffic. The trucks were loaded to their limits and moved rather slowly and noisily leaving black clouds behind in the air from their upright exhausts. During the night, these trucks left their lights on full beam so we had to be careful not to hit the holes on the side of the road. The road followed in a straight line to the horizon in this desert-like country.

Wooden power poles followed one side of the road. They were placed at equal distances and stood as straight as their natural growth allowed. This was a surprising sight.

A valley cut through rugged mountains to the Mediterranean coastal town of Adana. Barren, rocky mountains changed to lush green vegetation on the coastal plains around Adana. Palm trees gave this area an outstanding impression, like you would find in the tropics.

A heavy thunderstorm shortly after our arrival forced us to stop on higher ground. This deluge passed and the sun's regime made it very hot and sticky. It was obvious that the area had ancient connections with the Roman Empire. A well-conserved aqueduct of Roman origin before Skenderun reminded us of the historical importance of this area. Today oriental culture has taken over in places where people live and it has become a door to Arabic countries. As the temperature rose here considerably, we took precautions with our food intake and bought a large quantity of oranges. Mainly bread and cheese completed our daily menu. Big shipping installations in the harbour with a large military presence underlined the importance of Skenderun which was the destination of a main oil pipe from Iraq.

Syria

A steep mountain pass brought us closer to the Syrian border. The countryside along the coastline remained green. As soon as we headed inland from Tartous to Homs, the desert started to take over. We were now in Arabic heartland. The road to Homs for a short time crossed through Lebanese territory. There were border personnel, but no border control. Life in a Syrian town was more or less a copy of the one in Morocco. Everything happened under the watchful eye of Islam. Intensive sunlight dominated the day. Houses were built to keep the heat away with plenty of air circulation through doors and windows.

The roads were busy with people – all sorts of vehicles were constantly on the move. It appeared that while one part of this population was busy, another part rested and observed this hubbub. There were people demonstrating their skills with roadside stalls featuring jewellery, pottery and clothing. Salespeople pushed their wares with persistence. The shoe cleaner waited on the footpath to clean the dust off shoes.

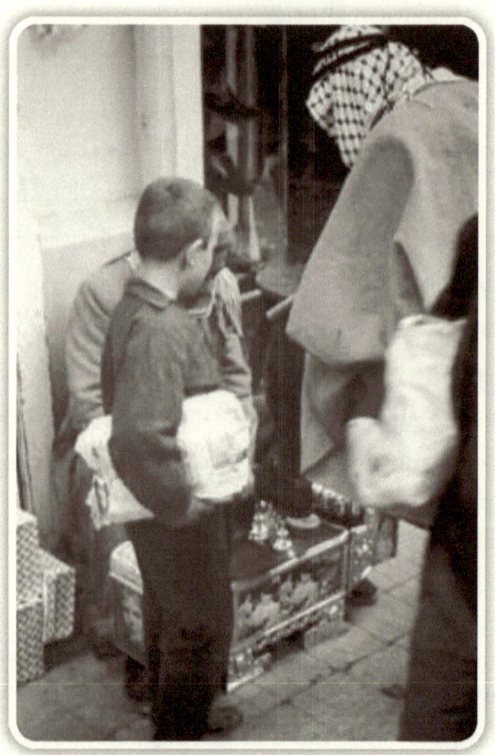
Shoe-cleaner, Damascus

Street-scene, Damascus

Everything was created individually according to material availability and bargaining power. All together this life reflected a colourful display of the Orient. The symbols of Islam stood out above all this – the high-domed mosque with its minaret-tower where the muezzin called for prayers.

The road to Damascus led through rugged desert terrain with huge rock formations called Golan Heights. In Damascus it seemed everyone was a salesperson. On one occasion, two young boys spoke to us in a few German words and invited us to their home. The whole family waited in the cooler rooms of their house to welcome us. They wanted to hear about Germany and served us soup for lunch around a big table. At the lunch end we were shown beautifully-made fabrics in golden thread called brocade. Not to disappoint our host too much, we bought only one or two pieces of souvenirs. We were not as rich as other tourists. Out of experience we knew how to barter. If you pay the amount the dealer asks for, you have spoilt the dealing exercise and paid way too much. You are better to offer a much smaller price first. The vendor now has to bargain for his money. There is a fine line in these negotiations where a vendor is satisfied and the customer has not paid too much.

All this bartering took time but we followed the local rules where you never show big money because there were always other eyes around watching.

We spent the rest of the day in the bazaars which were located mainly in the streets around the mosque. Omaijaden mosque with its ornament culture is different from others in the Islamic world. This is a reference to the diversity of religions in the Middle East. The site of the mosque featured ancient Roman temple foundations, a Christian basilica followed in the 4th century and in 705 to 715 Caliph Walid I built the mosque of today. In historical succession the Romans, Christians, Seldschukens, Mamlukens and Osmans had left their cultural marks here.

With advancing night we parked our Volkswagen-bus next to the post office building where we spent an undisturbed night with all the curtains closed inside our car. Life around us kept pulsing throughout the night but we did not experience any disruption from outside.

Lebanon

The next day we continued our tour into Lebanon. We had to cross the Anti Lebanon high mountain ranges to reach the border in a valley before the second Lebanon ranges began. The valley followed north to Baalbek, an ancient historical site where remnants of temple ruins date back to Greek civilisation, succeeded by Roman civilisation. There is grand scenery here – green pastures in the valley and white snow fields covered the surrounding mountains. Here were the oldest temples of Greek and Roman civilisations.

Baalbek

Today's contribution to a civilisation in this area appears insignificant judging by the settlement of Baalbek which is just outside the historical sites. We were the only visitors to Baalbek on that day and could not see any other foreigners.

A Lebanese family approached us and we were invited into their house. Our conversation was in French. Most elderly citizens still used to speak French because of the connection with France in the past. Two young ladies were also present. They were dressed in beautiful gowns, their round black eyes looking shy and deep black hair falling past their shoulders.

Over a cup of tea, the host couple asked us if we liked their daughters. We acknowledged that their two daughters were beautiful and we will remember this kind invitation. As poor students, we were not in a position to take the girls with us. Only after we had promised to write to them, could we make our goodbyes. The family was Christian and considered Germany a far distant wealthy country.

Lebanon stood out from many other Arabic countries because its women had a particular beauty and charm, relating to the diversity of cultures throughout history.

Here we learned a lesson that when we travel we cannot have all the beautiful things of this world!

Our tour continued towards Beirut. We had to cross the Lebanon, the second mountain range, which had a thick snow layer on its top. The road was cut through snow fields. Walls of snow rose high up on both sides of the road giving only a window view into the sky above.

Night had already fallen when we reached the outskirts of Beirut. We decided to stay outside of the city for the night and rest in our furnished bus in a place away from the main road. Our hosts in Baalbek had given us a bottle of Baalbek wine so we tried that wine that night. It was indeed an excellent wine.

When daylight broke, we realised that we had stopped beside a well-maintained orange grove along the hillsides before Beirut. The oranges shone through the dark green trees. They were so beautiful and plentiful that we could not resist having a taste. It was the Land of Promise for oranges – their deep orange colour, perfect oval shape, their size and sweet juicy taste – all this perfected after a long established culture in ideal climatic conditions.

After the snow in the mountains, the warm sunny weather welcomed us on the coast. Pulsing life with dense Mercedes traffic greeted us in Beirut. Life was a mixture of oriental impressions and European lifestyle. The central arterial road of this city ran down on a slope to the Mediterranean coast. Banks, shops, outdoor restaurants, sub-tropical gardens, innumerable vendors shouting their slogans – all this is why Beirut was named Paris of the Orient.

A young man, dressed in a European suit, approached us with his playing cards – only three of them. He placed the cards on a table outside a coffee house and started demonstrating his card trick showing the different possible number combinations. Just for interest we agreed to put a small amount of coins on the table. When we picked up the cards, they showed a different number combination and we lost our coins. He gave us the cards to shuffle and did the card trick again. My friend was curious so we had another go and lost again. We decided to abandon this game!

Beirut 1967

Our next move was to go to a travel agency to book a ship passage from Beirut to Alexandria in Egypt. A land passage through Israel was not possible from neighbouring Arabic countries. We had to bypass Israel to continue our tour. This sea passage for ourselves and our car was quite expensive but we thought we had secured the best possible deal. The days before our departure were spent exploring the area around Beirut with its rich ancient history. Before leaving Beirut, we tried to change money in a bank but were told that money exchange was only conducted with dealers in the street. Was this an agreement between the banks and the dealers?

We eventually changed our German marks into Lebanese pounds. We had to take time to find the best exchange rate.

We drove along the coast road to the north to Tripoli. The world's oldest town, Byblos, lies 40km from Beirut. Its ruins date back 2500BC. Every culture had left its marks here – Arabic, Roman and the Knights of the Cross. There were excavated rock walls, ruins of a temple and a castle and a small amphitheatre with a view into the Mediterranean. While relaxing in this ancient site, a young Lebanese boy came and kept us company. He invited us to visit his family. Here we entertained the host family with our guitar music. They were so impressed that they suggested to my friend that he takes one of their daughters. Under no circumstances we could accept such an offer even though my friend was quite taken with one of the beautiful daughters. I had to remind him that we were travelling together and it was time to move on. Cool heads prevailed and we left for Beirut with good memories.

Departure from Beirut

Egypt

Not much time was left to board the ship to Alexandria in Egypt. Our car was lifted, without incident, on to the ship under our watchful eyes. The ship was full with passengers. The weather was initially fine but then a severe storm hit and everybody became seasick. Huge waves rolled over the entire ship. It was difficult to imagine that the Mediterranean Sea could present such ferocious conditions in a relative small area. Should the ship have left Beirut at all? Was the German-built ship strong enough to go through a storm like this?

Everyone's seasickness turned the decks into a complete mess. Cabin beds with straps were the only way to secure ourselves and not be thrown around from the ship's extreme movements. After a stormy night, the sea settled in the morning hours.

It was totally calm and everybody tried to recover from this ordeal. Early in the afternoon of the following day, Alexandria turned up in bright sunshine. As soon as our ship had docked, a number of passengers could not wait to leave the ship over the gangway. Luggage was lowered with ropes everywhere along the ship to waiting people on the ground. Disembarkation lasted well into the night because of this hurry to leave the ship – everything was disorganised. People everywhere, nobody really knew who was a passenger and who was an Egyptian official.

Once we set foot on land, we were anxious to get our car safely on firm ground. Nobody could see who was in charge of this vehicle-lifting operation. We could see our car being lifted. Suddenly our car shifted in the air. Our hearts nearly stopped, but luckily it remained in a looped position. The touchdown on land in front of the ship shook us once more – the car's poor shock absorbers received the test of their life.

Patience finally helped us officially receive our car, but not before we had to sign for the car being in good order. This we really couldn't tell. We had to accept a change of number plates with Arabic letters in order to drive in Egypt. Our VW bus stood up to its reputation. Everything worked but the interior was a real mess because of the storm.

The temperature in the mighty Nile river delta was rather cold during night hours but this changed very quickly with the rising sun. We were well advised to hurry up with our car clean-up before the heat of the day arrived from the Sahara desert. Cairo was pulsing with traffic, people, donkeys and camels. Volkswagens were common in Egypt and, as our car was fitted with Egyptian number plates, it was not generally noticed that we were foreigners.

Our road led through a big oasis in the Nile delta. Everything around us reflected a variety of fresh greens. Water buffalos, oxen, cows, camels and donkeys grazed undisturbed between rice and sugar cane fields dotted with field workers. Men and women wore colourful long dresses, a head scarf for women was the rule here in the countryside. All life in Egypt unrolled along the banks of the river Nile which cuts its course through the arid lands of Western Sahara. All along this longest river in the world followed a band of lush green vegetation varying in its size. The Nile has been the lifeline of Egypt for thousands of years. Its water was channeled into fields everywhere. Water buffalos worked all day pushing a bar around in a circle to lift water into a higher channel with the help of a primitive construction called an Archimedes screw. Men also pushed on wooden levers with leather bags at either end to shift water to a higher level of the field.

Cairo, Egypt

Cairo

Time seemed to have stopped here. People lived their lives like they had done for thousands of years.

An image of our modern world could only be found in the capital of Cairo. This metropolis doesn't need to take a back seat with other large cities of the world. Nevertheless, its centre stood more out than its surroundings. Like all cities, it had a pulsing heart. People here had more freedom to choose their way of transportation. Buses were packed with people – some passengers hung outside the buses to get free transport. Everything went on a bus – people, baggage, chooks and pigs. A person entering a bus had to be on a constant lookout to get off the bus in time because they were so packed. There were not many passengers paying a regular fare because everything and everybody stood in one another's way. Taxis and trucks were equally used to their limits – every vehicle was packed with luggage and people.

If you were the first person to enter a taxi, you usually paid, allowing other people from around to fill up the taxi and have a free lift. A taxi not used to its full capacity was regularly stopped by people wanting cheap or free transport – subject to negotiations. There were so many Mercedes vehicles they were like an 'in-house brand'. No matter what age, they all were kept moving.

Mosques were an oasis of calm in this turmoil. Egypt was an Islamic State of Sunnites. The most direct descendants of ancient Egypt are the Copts. They are a Christian minority today. Arab descendants of the Bedouins lived mainly in the desert as nomads. The Fellahins were the majority of small farmers who lived in clay houses between fields along the river Nile.

Our first contact with locals was very friendly. They were more than happy to answer our enquiries to the best of their knowledge, even if they had to call others to join in. There were always many children around so we carried a variety of things, like colourful marbles and sweets, to give them. We did not give them coins.

A youth hostel in the centre of Cairo was our resting point from where we planned our excursions in and around the city. The ancient pyramid sites were not far from the western outskirts of Cairo.

Here in Egypt we experienced one major difference from home, toilets did not carry paper. Paper was considered too precious. Instead of paper, the toilet was fitted with a water pipe inside the bowl. To turn the pipe on you had to reach a tap on the wall. Such an exercise required some practice.

I visited the German Embassy to see whether Chris or Arja had sent a letter. There was one from Arja and I decided to read it later after we had left the restless life of the city.

Food was very basic for us (we were not staying at the Hilton). Very little was available: pilaw (meatballs), noodles, flat round bread, mutton and a selection of vegetables, that was it. We preferred to drink freshly-squeezed oranges, grapefruits or carrots juice as we could not drink the water. Buying goods was difficult because it was hard to change Egyptian pound notes. People had very little money. Even when we went to the official Volkswagen agency for spare parts, we saw how cheap their service was. We were given excellent service and a cup of coffee. This was the only place we received change for our notes. After this service we moved on to the pyramid site of El Giza. Camels waited to take tourists to the pyramids.

Cheops pyramid, El Giza

Chepren pyramid

Ascent inside Cheops pyramid

Empty tomb inside Cheops pyramid

Once you sat on a camel, you depended entirely on the local guide. This was not our plan, so we parked as close as was allowed to the pyramids and moved on by foot. Guards around had the task to direct visitors to the tour guides. We negotiated a deal so that we could inspect the site on foot.

The three pyramids stand on the edge of the Sahara desert where the Nile delta begins. They represent three epochs of ancient Egyptian Pharaohs in succession from north to south: Cheops, Chepren and Mycerinus of which Cheops is the mightiest.

Out of the guard's sight, I climbed the rock steps of Cheops pyramid right to the top. The sky was clear, a stiff breeze blew from the desert. The view was breath-taking. The endless sands of Sahara stretched behind me in yellow/brown colours. In front of me lay the deep green banks of the Nile and still further I could see the smog over the city.

I made sure to capture this view with my camera.

Stepping up 186 metres in the full heat of the day over rock steps requires a good fitness level. 'What goes up, also comes down' and so did I.

A steep passage on the foothills of the pyramid led to its interior – the tomb chamber. The air inside smelt incredibly musty and sticky. The walk went over timber planks with wooden strips across for better footing. We were on our own inside the pyramid. The lack of fresh air and the extreme heat made this exercise very difficult, not recommended for somebody with health problems. The empty tomb built out of massive rectangular granite boulders must have been a disappointment for many. The whole golden interior decoration with its mummy of Tut En Chamon had been removed and was exhibited in the Egyptian museum in Cairo. We paid it a visit after our excursion to the pyramids. The descent inside the pyramid back to the sandy ground on its front went faster than the ascent.

The huge Sphinx in front of the pyramid was completely fenced off. To get a decent photo of it, I had to convince a guard to open the fence for me. A tip helped in my negotiations.

To this day, we still cannot imagine how some 4500 years ago these huge granite blocks could be transported, not only all the way on the river Nile, but also from the river up to this elevation on the border of the desert. We cannot perform such tasks today. This was proven when the temple facades of Ramses II were shifted in Abu Simbel in Upper Egypt. The world wanted to save them from the flood levels of the Aswan dam which was being constructed. The colossus of granite statues had to be cut into sections in order to shift them to higher grounds.

When we left the pyramid site of El Giza and returned to Cairo, a sudden strong wind started to blow from the desert towards the city obscuring the whole sky with clouds of fine sand. The sun appeared only as a dark red disc in the sky. This was our first taste of a desert sandstorm. During that storm sand was everywhere. It even penetrated through the closed windows of the car and we felt the sand between our teeth. We had little choice, either the heat in the closed car or the flying sand from outside. After a few hours, the storm died down and with it the sand in the air disappeared. Very cold air had moved in for the night. Later on in Libya we experienced the real thing called a desert storm.

After a cold night, which is typical for desert conditions, we spent the morning of the next day in the Egyptian Museum. Taking photos was not allowed, especially the use of a flash. My camera let me take photos without the flash. The details I obtained in a few shots of a mummy behind a glass sarcophagus were unique. No such documentation exists anywhere.

Cheops tomb, Egypt. Museum

Mummy face, Tut En Chamon

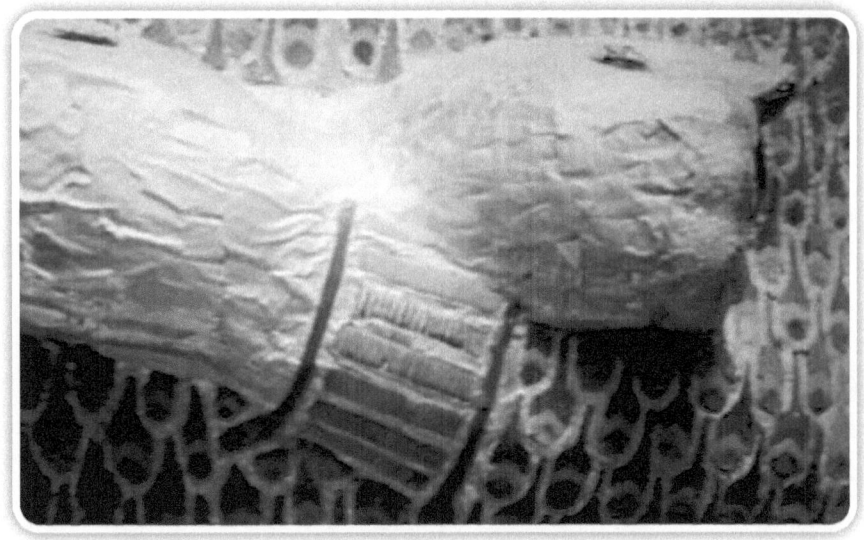

Mummy, hand – details

Mummy, robe – details

There were so many mummies exhibited in the museum that they lost their unique appeal after a while.

The other outstanding exhibit was the golden tomb chamber next to the golden mummy. These came from the empty chamber inside the pyramid that we had visited earlier.

After leaving the museum, we felt we had seen enough mummies for the time being.

Our trip continued from Cairo upstream along the river Nile. The deep green oasis followed on both sides of the river. The desert relentlessly took over where the irrigation from the Nile stopped. All life is connected to the river. Hamlets of clay-block houses knuckled under palm groves. Everywhere something grew – rice, sugar cane, bananas, oranges, lemons, cotton, olive trees and sweet, juicy onions which could be eaten like apples were widely traded.

Not far from Cairo, west of the Nile valley, was the oasis city of El Faiyum. The place was famous for its hydroponic culture of flowers which are used to extract the best perfumes. This is an ancient culture.

Ancient watering

Another watering

Archimedes – screw-watering

Sugar cane transport

Back on the road, we rested on the shores of the Nile overlooking life in the oasis. Now was the time to pull out the letter from the German Embassy in Cairo. Arja said she thought our tour was really special and she would have liked to have been a part of it. Her first careful approaches shined through in this letter I was so happy about it that even my friend noticed. I felt like 'new wings' had been added to our tour.

Our next destination was Asyut. Still the same picturesque scenery along the river with the difference being the green belt and its extensive cultivation started to get smaller.

A train track ran alongside the road. When a train came into sight it was a sight to behold. The passengers were not only in the carriages but on the roofs of the carriages. The 'top' passengers were obviously enjoying a free ride. We did not see anybody fall off the fast-moving train. Everything in Cairo was used to its maximum, whether it be a bus, taxi or river boat. These river boats had an appearance of their own: a low bow, a hull sitting wide and flat on the water and one big triangular sail in the centre of the boat with a bar in its bottom to direct the sail into the wind.

In Asyut we decided to leave the valley oasis and visit the Sahara desert.

The road to the west had a boom-bar across it with a large sign in Arabic letters, which we could not read. The boom was not locked, so we just lifted it up to give us a passage. The road narrowed but still showed some traces of bitumen. We had just reached the desert area when a woman suddenly appeared and signaled us to stop.

She was dressed in western-style and said in English: "I have to return to Charga Oasis where my husband and I are doctors at the local hospital. Can you give me a lift?" Charga Oasis was 250km away. We took her on board. During our drive she explained to us what she was doing. "Our government transferred my husband and myself to this hospital. We are restricted only to this place and are not allowed to leave but a family matter forced me to go secretly to Cairo. I am now on my way back."

The Sahara became an incredible experience. Steep canyons exposed colourful rock fields, plain yellow sand curled along plateaus, dark natural rock formations stood out like pyramids. Glaring sunshine was everywhere, not even one cloud in sight. In the middle of the day the temperature soared past 50 degree Celsius – our temperature gauge in the car stopped at a 50 degree reading. All the windows had to be kept open to allow the much-needed air circulation. The air was extremely dry.

Sahara desert

Sand-dune in Sahara

Our lady doctor co-passenger advised us to avoid dehydration. We had three boxes of oranges and our own boiled water.

We reached Charga Oasis within half a day expecting a green flourishing oasis but were greeted by a modern settlement with houses and roads right in the middle of the Egyptian Sahara. Charga Oasis was a pilot program of the government to settle people in the desert. Our co-passenger invited us into the hospital to meet her husband.

We were asked to inspect the hospital's international facilities. Light refreshments were offered during our short visit. One could easily forget we were here in a harsh desert territory.

The doctor couple escorted us back to the road. Our trip continued deeper into the desert. The road changed from now on. Sand dunes blocked the road – Dakkla Oasis lay ahead another 200km.

It took us hours to get around a sand dune. A shovel, planks and bags had to be brought into action which became extremely demanding in the heat. Nobody had to complain of perspiration because of the dry air. After each successful passage around a sand dune we crossed our fingers that this would continue for the rest of our journey.

Until then we had only heard of a mirage. Now we could see it on the horizon and take a picture. The air glittered in the heat above the ground mirages and made water surfaces appear – darker reflections from the ground formed images of a forest behind. Such images are created only from a specific distance. As soon as we came closer, the images started to fade. Mirages can be very confusing, especially for somebody finding himself in trouble in the desert.

The distance to Dakkla Oasis took us double the time than to Charga Oasis. Over the whole desert stretch we didn't meet any traffic – we were on our own. The green of the Dakkla Oasis came into sight within a depression of the desert landscape. The deep green belt announced life again. Before we could get there, armed guards came out of the roadside demanding us to stop. We had to leave our car and follow them to a checkpoint. Thus followed a very confusing and frustrating time. We could not communicate with the guards. We could only understand their native tongue.

Our situation appeared serious. They produced a box with plugs, wires and a handle. We had no idea what was going on.

The more they tried to call with their box, the louder they shouted. The heat of the day took its toll on us. The guards retreated every now and then to refresh themselves with watermelons. We eventually got them to understand that the doctors knew us back in Charga Oasis. Finally we were sent back to where we came from. The guards' determination to send us back was indicated by their machine guns. On our arrival at Charga Oasis we stopped at the hospital to say goodbye to the doctors. When they saw us again, they became very excited.

When the doctors learned of our trouble they said: "We thought you returned to Asyut. If we had known that you wanted to continue to Dakkla Oasis we had warned you not to do so. It is a prohibited area. Russia has installed underground rocket ranges. You are lucky to be alive. You could have been imprisoned. You did the right thing by giving them our names and we could put in a good word for you.

We are all glad it worked out. You helped my wife to come back to the hospital so we were more than happy to assist in getting you out of this dangerous situation."

After our cup of tea, we assured the doctors we would return to Asyut. They farewelled us and watched to make sure we headed in the right direction.

With nightfall we reached the Nile valley with its continuous oasis. We parked our van away from the main road which was always busy with people, camels and donkeys. This type of road traffic made it difficult for cars to pass – people and camels had the right of way. No other tourist was to be seen on the roads in Egypt. In those days, tourists mainly travelled by train or plane to visit the distant archaeological sights in Upper Egypt.

The road along the river Nile was subjected to rigorous police controls at the beginning and end of each settlement.

All the people we met were friendly. In one village we had a remarkable experience. Young boys welcomed us as we drove into the settlement. As soon as we stopped, people came out of clay houses from all directions. The houses were hidden in palm groves and sugar cane fields. An elderly man came towards us, shook our hands and asked us to sit with him in front of his house. He appointed a number of men to look after our car. He spoke some English. After hearing where we came from, questions poured out like cascades. He also translated our conversation to the people around. Tea arrived from other houses. We gave some presents mainly to the younger generation. Before leaving this friendly meeting we had to promise to send a picture postcard from Germany. Our visit was a special event for these people. All of them farewelled us and some followed our car as we left the settlement.

Luxor waited for us further upstream. It was here that we met other tourists for the first time and saw some souvenir shops and hotels. The local police had many arguments with us about our car tour through Egypt. They probably would have liked to see us travelling by air or train, like all the other tourists. We succeeded in calming the police officers.

Egypt at that time kept a tight control over its population. The checkpoints in the settlements must have been in place to keep control over population movements. People like our lady doctor were restricted to their workplace. Tourists like us also had to obey the settlement controls.

It appeared that Egypt did not want foreigners to 'infiltrate' their country, leaving everything the way it had been for thousands of years. The positive side of this was that we could travel in parts of Egypt that were still like they were thousands of years ago, back in the days of the Pharaohs.

In Luxor, we found accommodation in a youth hostel where we met some other tourists who had all arrived by train.

The ancient temples of the historic Thebe were located in the west on the opposite banks of the river. To get there we had to use the ferryboat across the Nile. At first we tried to take our car with us, but when the ferryboat operators almost dropped our car into the river, we changed our minds very quickly. Our car remained in Luxor.

During this incident with our car, we met a German couple amongst the crowd of local Egyptians. When our car was being mishandled, a 'good' German swearword slipped past my lips. The German couple was the only ones out of the crowd to understand and they burst out laughing.

The German couple remained on the ferryboat while we stored our car. Before we left, they invited us to the Hotel Luxor that night.

When we arrived across the river, we found out that we could rent bicycles.

The scenery in front of the Valley of the Kings included Amun temple with colossal reliefs showing the battle against the Hethiter. There was a column court, three from six remaining monumental statues of Ramses. There was one obelisk. Originally there were two, but the second then stood in the Place de la Concorde in Paris.

Valley of the Kings

Ramses statues

A steep wall of rocks dropped off from a higher plateau of Sahara desert to the lower ground that sheltered the ruins of a temple of the Egyptian King. Wide rock steps led to a platform in this desert canyon with incomplete pillars pointing to temple constructions.

In front of these temple ruins lay massive piles of rock. Climbing one of them, we gained a good view. One pile had an entrance which had probably been blocked by natural causes. We headed down to this spot and had to move some rocks and soil to find the entrance to a corridor. We were very cautious as we didn't want to be buried alive in a crumbly corridor. Just 10 to 15 metres inside from the entrance we discovered on the wall pictures in vivid colours of the God Osiris surrounded by reliefs. The representations were in perfect condition.

I managed to get photos of our discovery despite the dim lighting. We were overwhelmed from these findings. We left the corridor and replaced the soil and rocks at the entrance. We never told anyone about our find. It would be interesting to find out if this site has since been discovered. Our photos are proof that my friend and myself discovered this ancient Egyptian site on March 30, 1967. These photos are in this book to support our claim.

Tomb-site discovery

Not many people can claim such a discovery. The undisturbed condition of the site was directly responsible for its good preservation. For that reason we left it exactly as we had found it.

To meet up with the German couple at the Hotel Luxor that night, we had to return and cross the river again. We carried one set of good clothing for special occasions and we dressed in these outfits that night. It turned out to be a great night. The Hotel Luxor was one of the best in town but it was not very generous with its dinner servings. Good conversation made up for this. The host couple travelled in their own aircraft. They operated a very successful business in Stuttgart which supplied the whole world with equipment for hobby fishtanks. Hardly any other guests were in the large open dining rooms of the hotel. The hotel was so big that we nearly felt lost.

We had an early evening so that we could all get up early for a boat trip on the Nile. Next morning we joined our host couple on a local boat which the Fellahins used to transport crops to the markets. The heat of the day was tolerable on the boat in the early hours. Our Egyptian boatman used the big triangular sail to move our boat quietly and steadily on the river's calm surface. We took our guitar on board and played from the higher position of bow. The sound of the guitar moved with the air past the sail. We all enjoyed a couple of relaxing hours in bright sunshine.

Back in Luxor, we exchanged home addresses with the promise to keep in touch. The German couple told us about Abu Simbel, a place they had visited in their aircraft – the only way to get there as there were no roads. Here the temple monuments were being moved to a higher position because they would have been flooded by the new Aswan Dam which was under construction near Aswan, some 400km downstream. The temple facades of Ramses II were near completion from being moved 65 metres higher up to a new position. The huge granite figures of the king and the queen as a sitting and standing couple had been cut into segments in order to move them to their new location. Three days earlier we could have joined the German couple in their aircraft, so sadly we missed out on experiencing Abu Simbel.

The German couple flew back to Germany and we continued with our tour to Aswan. The road changed dramatically. On a dusty stone road we only met camels transporting sugar cane. The cane was strapped right around the camel's body. This load claimed the entire width of the road. We had to stop on the rocky side to allow these 'ships of the desert' to continue their passage. The camels would not move out of the way and there was a risk that they would be frightened by a car. So we always stopped in time and for this gesture the camel drivers returned a friendly nod.

The oasis along the river began to shrink here. Steep rocky slopes from the desert came closer to the river leaving no room for agriculture.

Just before Aswan, the road changed to a partly bitumen surface. I must mention here about the amount of flies in the upper valley of the Nile. They were always our company and we needed a good dose of insect spray to gain some relief.

In Aswan the modern Egyptian civilisation ended, only the ancient culture moved further south upstream to Abu Simbel.

Besides being the site for the new super-dam, Aswan was also known as having the highest natural radioactivity on earth and being a place where it never rains.

Started obelisk in a quarry

It was here that the ancient cultures of Egypt extracted the huge granite rocks that were used to build the pyramids in El Giza. The long columns of the obelisks came out of a quarry near the river, where we could still see an unfinished obelisk. Slaves spent years cutting around the rock with hammers and chisels. They dug a trench around a column shape, leveling the top first, then the two sides. How they cut the huge granite column from underneath out of the rockbed, nobody knows today. This pink/black spotted granite is one of the hardest rocks in the world.

The work that went into an obelisk, as we can see them today in Egypt, Paris and London, was so enormous especially when we consider the perfect straightness and smooth surfaces of an Egyptian obelisk.

I know measurements were taken with today's technology that proved the accuracy of the ancient stonemason's workmanship.

The results were extraordinary. Today we cannot reproduce this quality.

We should not forget that a human cost was also involved to create the cultural expressions of ancient Egypt!

What is a culture? One side comes up with an idea, other sides work with great efforts and very often with sacrifices to bring the idea to reality. Can cultural expressions justify this sacrifice?

In Aswan we reached the southern culmination of our tour in Egypt. The construction of the new Aswan dam was headlines around the world. Russia built this monstrous construction a few kilometres upstream from an existing dam. We caught a glimpse of the construction site. Between two gigantic stone and soil hills started the concrete construction of sky-rocketing pillars for the future dam wall.

The new Nasser lake stored the water of the Nile 600km upstream into the territory of Sudan. Water and power were the benefits of such a project. An unforseen side-effect of this great project was soon evident.

Before the dam stopped the flow of the Nile, regular floods delivered fertile mud onto its banks enabling farmers to benefit from such natural fertilization. Today this dam holds all this fertile mud back. Egypt has started, like the rest of the world, to apply synthetic fertilizers resulting in heavy pollutants entering the river system.

This impact on the environment and population appears to be 'kept under the carpet'. This is nothing new: for every benefit we create, we also create problems. We chose a different route back to Cairo.

Traffic in Upper-Egypt

After a while travelling back on the stony dust road we turned off at Idfu towards the Red Sea. What a surprise, this road had a new bitumen layer! We crossed into mountainous desert country. The heat during the day became unbearable. Many camel skeletons pointed to the extreme conditions.

A well near the road supplied water only in a case of an emergency. We did not bother to take any of this uncertain water on board.

As soon as we reached Marsa Alam on the Red Sea coast, a cooler breeze welcomed us. Here the desert drops directly into the sea. Not even one plant could be seen. In contrast to the desert, a rich sea life was established here. Beautiful shells of all sizes waited on the sandy beach to be picked up. We were lucky that we did collect specimens because they later served as bartering items when we became low on funds.

Only a few people lived here in huts which were partly built out of materials thrown overboard from ships. We collected wooden boxes for our cooking. Only once we tried to get closer to the water by driving through the sand but then we had to work for half a day to get back to the road.

Far in the east, the desert mountains of Saudi Arabia lined the horizon. The water of the Red Sea was over 30 degrees. We refrained, however, from swimming because of jelly fish in the water.

One stranded timber box attracted our attention. It was in such good condition that we could even read the name of the ship and the place where it came from – Glasgow. This box was kept in the car to store our shells.

The monotonous desert along the Red Sea changed only when we got closer to Suez, the entrance to the busy channel which connects to the Mediterranean Sea. It was here that we encountered a fantastic sea-world display – Egyptian style.

Over the shallow water of the beach, timber planks were used for walkways to get as close as possible to the sea creatures which were kept in separate underwater tanks. There were sharks, octopuses, corals, wonderfully coloured fish, manta rays and sting rays.

We were the only visitors at that time. When we got back in the car, we saw a big sign pointing to an 'Ocean Museum'. We were not sure whether this was the underwater tanks, so we asked some locals. Before we could finish our question, one boy opened the side door of our van and a second later everybody else from the road was in our car. We could not communicate with them. They just expressed their happiness to be with us and pointed to the front indicating the direction they wanted to go. What should we do? We could only listen to their constant noisy Arabic clatter. Not long after, our car 'told' us that it could not carry the weight of these people any longer. We stopped, opened the side door and made it clear that they had to leave our car. The party was over!

From then on we made sure our doors remained locked while driving.

Around Ras Gharib a small crude-oil resource of Egypt appeared with derricks in this desert landscape. Pipelines lay unarranged on the ground. They must have had leaks because there was an intense smell of oil across the entire area. It was in our own best interests to move out of this area.

Soon after a dust road branched off into the Arab desert. The fortress of a Coptic monastery, St. Paulus, was located in total solitude 12km further. High stone walls isolated this monastery from the rugged mountainous desert. No life was first visible in this merciless environment.

From a tower hung a rope to swing a bell. Visitors announced their presence this way. It took a while until somebody attended our call. A man dressed in a brown hooded robe appeared in an opening high up in the tower and then disappeared. We thought he had ignored us but soon after a small, squeaky side door opened slowly. The man from the tower stood in front of us and invited us to come in. What a different world we saw here! A palm grove surrounded the centre of an inner yard with cultivated crops and vegetables.

St. Paulus – monastery

A fountain bubbled constantly, its water flowing through a channel system. The fountain was skirted by wrought iron fences.

St. Paulus is the oldest Christian monastery and its fountain has been its lifeline for all those years.

Two church rooms were located within the inner wall. A shelter was built for each of the 20 permanent monks as well as a complete library. The monks took us on a tour of the monastery. The monks spoke neither English nor French so our communication was very difficult. Besides Arabic, they also spoke Hebrew, ancient Greek and Latin. We tried our schoolboy Latin to the best of our ability.

We were invited to join the monks for a cup of tea and this gave us the chance to meet all the monks. They were dressed in different coloured, hooded robes. Each monk made an individual impression.

The time came for the monks to resume their regular religious duties so we bade farewell. The monks returned to their solitude in the monastery.

St. Paulus monks

The dust road through rugged mountainous desert brought us back on to the bitumen road along the coast of the Golf of Suez. The closer we came to the Suez channel, the more ships waited in the Gulf for their passage. The rocky mountain walls of the Sinai peninsula stand on the other side of the Gulf. The sea's surface was totally calm.

We collected some broken wooden boxes to help with our campfire.

The Suez channel was built under the French supervision of F. Lesseps in 1859. The project took more than 10 years. Today it is still the most important shipping route as it is the shortest passage between East and West. During the time of its construction, malaria decimated large numbers of construction workers. The concentration of interests in this passage sparked various conflicts.

Only a few weeks after being in this area, the Six-Day War broke out between Israel and Egypt when Israel claimed the Sinai peninsula with the eastern side of the Suez channel. Shipping resumed again in 1975 after Egypt won control rights over the Suez channel.

The calm we encountered in the region was in real terms a 'calm before the storm'. We were lucky not to get caught in such a storm. The flat countryside made the big ocean ships look like they were moving in the desert. The Suez channel passes through an inner sea called the Bitter Sea. This area, during the construction of the channel, was the breeding grounds for malaria. The channel is a clean-cut waterway through this isolated desert east of the Nile delta oasis.

El Alamein, German – flack

To continue our tour without delay, we bypassed Cairo by taking the road to Alexandria. We must have somehow foreseen the imminent conflict here.

El Alamein was the next town at the Mediterranean Sea. In the flat sandy desert stood three cemeteries belonging to three nations. It was a stark reminder of the fierce battles between three nations. What sense did these countless numbers of white crosses make here in a desert? The English cemetery was here. Two German tanks and a number of cannons were buried in the sand as well. A book gave visitors an opportunity to write about their experience.

Further down the road was the memorial to fallen German soldiers. A clean-joined stone wall in a polygonal form rose from the desert near the coast. An entrance leads inside to inscriptions of the names of fallen soldiers and a reminder never to repeat such a conflict. Italy had built a tower close by to remember their sacrifices.

Libya

Repair work on our car delayed our progress that day so it was in the middle of the night that we arrived in the border town of Soloum on the foothills of a high plateau where Libya begins. Before continuing the steep road to the plateau we exchanged our Egyptian pounds into petrol cans. Only when we continued our trip did we realise that the cans were leaking, they spilled petrol in our car. We had to leave the cans behind in the desert. As if this was not enough, the border control insisted on an inspection and sent us back to the office. When we returned everything was shut so we decided to call it a night and get some sleep.

The next morning we had to wait until somebody turned up at the border office. We had to contend with a lot of paperwork before receiving the green light to continue our trip. Before we left, we could not resist the offers to exchange some of our goods for their special souvenirs like an Arabic silk ring which goes over the head to secure a headscarf. As soon as one dealer attended us, others joined in from everywhere.

While trying to escape from the place, another VW bus turned up parking next to us. Two young men of our age from Switzerland got out of the car. The dealers turned to these new arrivals, before we could leave. The Swiss fellows had the obvious intention to buy, not to sell. The dealers, however, wanted to find out what they carried with them. When I saw the Swiss driver openly display his firearms, I knew it was time to leave. Trouble was on the cards.

The border controls on the Egyptian side up on the plateau were relatively quick.

We did not have to look far for the Libyan border which consisted of rolls of barbed wire and a tiny hut with two guards in dark-green uniforms. We stopped our car next to the entrance door. The guards waited in the hut while we emptied all our belongings out of the car. The relationship between President Nasser's Egypt and the Kingdom of Libya was obvious here. The border guards' demands did not impress us at all. I wanted to take a photo of the guards and lined up a shot of our belongings piled up in front of the hut. Just when I took a photo, one of the guards yelled something. I quickly walked back to the car and exchanged my good camera for my old one. When I turned from the car I felt a cold, hard point on my back – it was the end of a machine gun barrel.

I had to do everything right and convince the guard not to pull the trigger. I was pushed into the hut with the machinegun in my back. Arriving in front of a desk, the second guard requested my camera. He grabbed it and tried to open it in vain. He indicated to me to open the camera for him. He quickly pulled the film out and held it towards the light from the open door. Showing satisfaction, the guard handed back the camera with the spoiled film. I still had the machinegun in my back so I did not make any comment. With hand signs and friendly mimes I made it clear that there was no reason to point the gun at me anymore. The message slowly sunk in. The atmosphere returned to normal and the machinegun was put down. I was very relieved.

The guards allowed us to to return our belongings to the car. The trip continued with the photo in question in the other camera.

Before Tubruq, we experienced delays because of massive road constructions.

A real autobahn was being built. Gigantic earth-moving machines created dust clouds in the air. The sun disappeared and the spotlights had to be switched on. All the construction workers wore complex filter masks. The site was turned into an alien world. Oil pipelines were laid above the ground in straight lines and followed to the road.

A sign said the installation company was Mannesmann from Germany. The oil had created wealth here.

The town of Tubruq was a modern construction of concrete buildings and shops lining the streets. At last we could buy what was needed!

Nobody was interested in foreign currency here – a stark contrast to other countries we had passed through. The Libyan pound was a very strong currency and we could only change our German money in official banks. Life in Libya appeared much different from life in Egypt. There were no obtrusive dealers nor begging children along the sides of the road. In Egypt some of these dealers and beggars would throw stones at you if they were not satisfied. There were two main reasons why this didn't happen in Libya. Firstly, Libya had a much lower population density because of the harshness of its desert surroundings. Secondly, Libya had wealth from its vast oil resources. The recent oil boom enabled Libya to lift its living standards.

Tubruq is another memorial place from World War Two. A copy of Egypt's El Alamein is a reminder of the ferocious battles held here and how many lost their lives.

After Tubruq, we climbed a plateau called Jabal al Akdar. Now in spring time, this area was transformed into a garden of Eden. In green meadows camels grazed with their young, spikes of grain waved in fields, small patches of green forests stopped the dominance of the Sahara.

The road descended again to the coast through Wadi El Kuf, a bizarre rock valley. The Wadi had eroded a huge washout along its rock-wall banks. A high bridge led across to an alpine serpentine road. It was a picture of the unexpected diversity of the Sahara.

Benghazi is Libya's second largest city. The traffic was different from Egypt. Oncoming traffic in Libya stopped all the time, while nobody stopped in Egypt. Has this something to do with the different population density? The Egyptian style of driving can be found in today's China where everybody smiles and takes the right-of-way. First come, first served is the rule.

A bad road with large sections of construction work slowed our progress down. There was hardly any traffic on this coastal road. In the distance we saw a car stuck in the sand. It looked very much like ours except for the colour. Coming closer, we realised the car belonged to the two Swiss fellows we had met on the Egyptian border.

The car looked abandoned. All the windows were smashed and there was no trace of the owners. As soon as we saw them show off their guns, we were afraid that something like this would happen. Somebody must have followed them and confronted them – most likely at night. The car was already disappearing into the moving desert sand. What happened to the two Swiss men was anybody's guess.

Near Sirte we had car trouble. We arrived in Sirte and to be greeted by a horrific sandstorm. No banks or shops or garages were open. We continued driving through the sandstorm, stopping every so often to top up the oil level of the right back wheel's bearing housing.

We didn't get far though and had to stop and camp for the night. When we checked the car we were disappointed to find that the wheel bearings in the back wheel had completely collapsed and were beyond repair. The closest place to get a spare part was in Tripoli – 500km to the west.

We tossed a coin to determine who went to Tripoli and who stayed with the car. I was chosen to go to Tripoli.

Just off the main road I got a lift with a driver in a Mercedes cross-country truck. The driver spoke fluent English. He was from Switzerland and also spoke German. We didn't travel far because all the traffic had stopped to sit out the sandstorm. I was lucky that I could stay in the truck cabin during this storm. The cabin had a kitchen and a sleeping facility. The truck protected us from the heat and the sand very well.

Romano, the driver, prepared spaghetti for the night and invited me to join him. I spent the night on the comfortable passenger seat.

Early the next morning, the sandstorm had died down. After a cup of coffee, we continued our trip to Tripoli.

Romano told me about his life of 35 years in the desert supplying oil drill stations with technical equipment. He owned the truck and was his own boss. He said his trips through the desert were always challenging with the constant changing landscape of the desert, mainly through sandstorms, making orientation very difficult. Only experienced people could enter the interior of Sahara desert. Romano was a generous man who helped his family back in Switzerland and lots of other people. He was unhappy though, that his isolated job had prevented him from finding a wife. I told Romano that he should believe that his wishes would one day come true.

Getting closer to Tripoli, the sandy desert started to change into a green oasis with palm forests and fields of crops. This was some 150km before the city on a road that was close to the sea. Again it was obvious that water was the key to life. All desert grounds are rich in minerals and ancient traces of nutrients – they just need water to spring into life.

There were more and more shops and restaurants as we came closer to Tripoli. Romano stopped at a restaurant and suggested we have a farewell meal together. Everybody knew him at the restaurant and he was communicating fluently in Arabic with the locals. The restaurant had no menu, meals were negotiated. We enjoyed a mixture of Arabic and Italian food. We were the only guests.

It was Friday afternoon and time to make our way into the city. Romano dropped me off at the Volkswagen service shop and, with a firm handshake, we said goodbye.

Unfortunately the VW shop had closed just half an hour before. I realised I would have to stay the weekend and wait for the shop to open on Monday.

I enquired at a nearby hotel but it was too expensive. I had no choice but to look for somewhere else. But there were not many options in this big city with wide roads and plenty of modern buildings. In the end I made my way to the beach where there was a park and benches – not far from the royal palaces. I did not sleep well on the hard bench and in the night cold of the desert. I thought: "Who would want to rob a tramp in this part of the world?" When morning came, the sunshine brought back much-needed warmth.

I freshened up at a fountain near the royal palaces. I filled my weekend by walking around the city, its parks and beaches. There were many locals at the beach but I didn't see any of them go into the water. Usually shops opened on the weekend in Tripoli, but I was very unlucky to have arrived in this city when the Muslims were celebrating a religious event and so every business activity had to stop.

I also visited a museum next to the royal palaces. Entrance was free because of the religious festivities. The museum featured the Libyan desert and had many stuffed animals on display. They looked so real. The dry climate must have helped such excellent preservation.

On Monday morning I waited in front of the VW shop but it did not open. After a while I saw two men of non-local appearance in the building. They told me that the shops would stay closed until Tuesday because of the religious celebration. As it turned out, the two men were from Germany. They invited me to their house. They were delighted to have a visitor from their native country. We shared food and German beer all day. They told me they were working in Tripoli on contract with VW.

During the day, other locals arrived and stayed for a chat. Besides general conversations, we also discussed the current situation in Libya. The King stayed in Tubruq where he enjoyed the protection of the English military. American interests controlled the oil resources of the country. Libya found itself in the firm grip of foreign control. Also, Libya was under the watchful eye of Egypt which did not have many oil resources. And, Egypt's leader, Nasser, was well aware that Libya had a much smaller population than Egypt. Nasser was ambitious – it was he who sent the King of Egypt packing. The next in line could have become the King of Libya. Egypt was providing teachers to Libya in preparation of establishing a greater Egyptian influence in the country.

During our stay in Libya, the American Air Force staged training sessions across the desert for the Vietnam War. This was the background to the rise of Ghaddaffi who ousted the King just two years after our visit. He restored Libya as a country in its own right.

While he made a number of mistakes during this time of takeover and clean-up, Ghaddaffi did save Libya's identity, no matter what side of politics you are on.

Meanwhile, the party continued at my German hosts' house and we soon decided to visit a 'hidden' nightclub. The venue was 'hidden' because we were in a Muslim country. Even though I was very tired, I agreed to go to the nightclub. The Greek girls who staged the show eventually kept me awake. Whisky was served – all paid for by my hosts. These drinks also kept me awake. We eventually returned home in the early morning hours. There was hardly any time left to sleep – I fell asleep just when it was time to get up for the working day. After a joint breakfast, we all headed to the VW depot in the city centre.

The workshop was open at last. A number of Italian motor mechanics also worked there. The foreign workers were employed primarily to train the locals who were good and willing workers.

Finally somebody found the bearing I needed plus all other possible parts I might need. As soon as I had paid for my parts, I started my trip back to my friend. Some transport had been organized for me for the first leg of the journey. It only took two lifts to complete the trip. On the final one, I joined an Arabic sheikh in his Mercedes 600. The car had every imaginable luxury on board – climate control, television, telephone and fridge.

The sheikh handed one German beer after another during the trip. He was delighted to have a German citizen on board. I did not drink all the beer cans – I stored some in my jacket for my friend who had spent five lonely days patiently waiting with the van.

I arrived back just before dusk. Our car was covered in desert sand with only the roof sticking out. Where was my friend?

I started to clear sand away from the side door. I looked through the window but couldn't see any trace of my friend. What I saw instead was a piece of paper fixed to the table with some kind of scribble visible. I got the door open and read the message. I was angry. My friend had written that it appeared I was incapable of organizing parts for our car so he had taken a bus to Tripoli to get the parts himself. He had used some of our limited funds to buy the bus ticket. All he achieved when he arrived at the VW shop was the message that I had already left with the parts. He had certainly heard about the delay. It was only a couple of hours later that my friend returned on the bus. It gave me enough time to cool down and not be so angry. When he arrived he put on a big smile, aware that he had made a mistake.

Nightfall didn't give us the time to discuss anything further. We decided to leave this incident behind us and get back to the business of fixing our car – and digging it out of the sand. In less than two hours the car was out of the sand and back on the road.

Only then I revealed to my friend the existence of the German beer cans that I had collected during the last leg of my trip. All the bad blood was instantly forgotten – a delicious beer helped to restore the old good friendship.

A touchstone in difficult life situations can tell us a lot about a person's character. Now was not the time to be judgmental. Better to forget what happened and pull together to continue our journey. We should always learn from difficult situations.

Our trip through the night took us as far as Misratah. Our car was running well. We stopped before sunrise to have a good rest and then bought some food for breakfast from the local stores.

Arriving in Tripoli, we visited our German friends at the VW shop and then arranged for the police to issue us with entry visas so that we could leave the country. It was our German friends who advised us to get the visas – without their help we would have had to make a return trip to Tripoli in order to get across the border. They invited us to stay the weekend but it was April 14 and time was running out – we had to be home by the end of the month.

Our journey continued under a cloud-free sunny Libyan sky. Leaving Tripoli was a 'piece of cake'. At the Tunisian border, the Libyan border control guards had another go at us. Two Libyan locals were waiting at the border office wanting to get a lift. The guards ordered us to take the two locals with us but we had to refuse because of our car's low-powered engine. The guards didn't understand our explanation and so ordered us to empty our car for a closer inspection. They obviously had more time than we did. They could not find anything suspicious but took a liking to our Red Sea shell collection. We gave them some shells and this gave us a more pleasant clearance. Meanwhile the two other passengers had lost their patience and had moved away. The guards welcomed our Arabic farewell.

Tunisia

The Tunisian border controls were straight forward with no dramas. Here the landscape started to change. Hillsides interrupted flat desert land and green vegetation gained a foothold. Large olive groves covered entire sections of the country. It was obvious that the influence from the French colonial times was a positive one. The farmers had learned to continue cultivating the new and existing crops.

Tunisia had changed to a secular society. Islam was still the dominant religion besides a Christian catholic minority which dated back to the French occupation. Women didn't have to wear a head scarf, everybody was dressed in a more European way. In the small settlements along our way, children in school uniforms played in the streets. An orderly life was enjoyed here.

Tunisia did not have the 'black gold' of Libya, people here worked more for their living. Farm labourers could be seen everywhere on well-established fields. Further north, wine fields added to the scenery. A garden country welcomed us here. After so many days in desert environment, this became a journey through paradise. People had transformed the semi-desert into a blossoming garden.

It was only natural to park our car overnight in an orange grove – the shiny fruit was too inviting. There were orange trees across hills as far as the eye could see. Cicadas sent their chirping in waves through the cooler air of a new nightfall. We were left undisturbed, surrounded only by a mixed odour of fresh soil, orange leaves and their fruit.

The next morning we were not in a hurry to leave before sunrise. The road to the capital Tunis was in an excellent condition all the way. Arriving there we went to the Embassy of Algeria and lodged our visa applications.

The embassy staff looked at our passport pictures, then at us again because we looked quite different with our beards. They insisted we have new photos in our passports and so we had this rectified. This meant that for the remainder of the trip we could not change our appearance and shave our beards. We had to wait a couple of days for our visas to be rubber stamped. While driving through the dense city traffic, we came beside another VW van with German number plates.

Both vehicles stopped and a conversation got underway. The other travellers were German engineers working in the country. They told us that they were given their van a few days earlier by two German tourists. The tourists were going to abandon the vehicle because it was not running properly – even though they were car mechanics! It didn't take the two engineers long to fix the vehicle.

After more conversation, we were invited to stay with the Germans in their house. On the way there we met another German man and his Swedish girlfriend. They were short of money and asked us to help them – but we couldn't. This was not an isolated incident. On other occasions we were also confronted with down-and-out travellers. Any help in such a case would not achieve much because once such a low point is reached, everybody else could become part of this 'sinking boat'. We could not afford to risk our own safety.

Arriving late in the afternoon at the engineers' house, we were offered our own room with two beds. A bed was pure magic! We hadn't slept in a bed for weeks – just the hard platform in our van.

Our hosts were also enthusiastic chefs and we enjoyed our evening meal immensely. Our hosts then invited us to join them at a special function the next day – by official invitation of Tunisia's President Bourguiba. Our hosts were quick to offer their additional black suits for us to wear. Not bad at all, we thought. After breakfast, everybody dolled up in their suits.

The casino venue welcomed an assembly of government officials and a large number of German aid workers. Our presence was thus unnoticed – we blended in perfectly. A slogan above the casino entrance said: "God save Bourguiba the sponsor of German-Tunisian friendship".

There was an interesting mix of personalities at the function. Qualified German aid workers worked for a relatively low income in the country. They only received a bonus after returning to Germany.

Officially, none of these ladies and gentlemen were in possession of a car because they were not encouraged to display wealth. Despite this, everybody had a car but with German number plates.

Speeches were held mainly in the French language. A big lunch with local wines and German beers helped to restore our wellbeing. An organised bus tour offered a free taste of all the locally-grown fruits. It is a pity the fruits in our shops at home were all picked 'green' and we never saw fully-ripened fruit on display. Afterwards the group got together in a sports ground for a cultural festival. Locals danced with swords while standing on the back of horses. A traditional couscous dinner was served in tents on the boundary of the festival. Dances followed in the open performed by young female dancers in their colourful costumes. A silk ring secured a clay jug atop their heads which they held with one hand while performing skilled dance movements. Young men in traditional dress performed quicker dance movements than the women. Music was played on Tunisian flutes accompanied by drums. The music sounded oriental with its short, constantly-changing rhythms.

Tunisian festivity

The bus tour continued to the coast where many hotels were being built near the cliff-top road. This complex of hotels being built on this magnificent Mediterranean coastline signalled that the country was preparing for many more tourists to help get their economy off the ground. The festival ended before sunset. We were very pleased to have been given the chance to experience a special day on a Tunisian events calendar.

The rest of the day was spent with other guests in the hosts' house in the suburb of La Goulette. Plenty of German beer was offered again.

One of the guests, a gentleman in his forties, also came from 'Dracula country' (Transylvania) and he was impressive with his local knowledge and stories. He sold expensive coffee machines in desert areas beyond the Tunisian border. He was the perfect salesman and even sold coffee machines to people who did not have water, coffee or power! He offered his customers a view into a future, convincing them they could make a business out of serving coffee. Many of his customers were attracted by the machines' shiny metal parts. A business with water, coffee and power didn't worry them that much, they were more excited about being the proud new owners of a shiny machine. The objectives of a sale were always reached with both parties happy.

The next morning reality dawned again. Our hosts had to go to work and we had to continue our trip home.

Before leaving we exchanged some of our shell collection for much-needed money. By midday we had our visas stamped and we were ready to enter Algeria.

Algeria

It did not take long to get to the border because Tunisia is a rather small country compared with its neighbours Libya and Algeria. Hills changed into mountains the closer we came to the border. The good road was left behind in Tunisia. A toll-bar across the road stopped our progress. Nobody could be seen at first until a man walked out of a field which backed on to a forest. He walked to the small customs house and got dressed in his official uniform. He then started talking to us in French. Rather than focusing on border control issues, we talked along personal lines. Not long after, a second guard turned up. The guards were about our age and were pleased to meet us.

During our conversation, a strange noise came through the door of an adjacent room. When we asked what was behind the door, the guards started to laugh and cautiously opened the door.

Grunting piglets in their typical stripes rushed through the gap of the door, but there was no sow in sight. The guards were quick to explain: "We shot the sow this morning in the forest and, as it turned out, she was pregnant with this lot." We held our breath and wondered how this could have happened. Maybe the guards were spinning a yarn. Anyway, they were happy to clear us through the border and we continued on our way.

We were now faced with the problem that there were few road signs in this isolated area. And if there was one, we could not read the Arabic letters.

The road after the border improved only gradually. As night took over, we had to stop to end the confusion of the day. We couldn't sleep well so decided to keep going. In the middle of the night there was no traffic.

It was a miracle to find the right road at a junction. At a railway crossing the gate was shut, but no train arrived. A light came on in a nearby cabin and the gate keeper opened the gate in his pyjamas – closing it again straight after us. Wasn't this an interesting way to control the traffic? Which one asked for more attention, the train or the vehicles? According to this gatekeeper, the train was more important. He would rather stop traffic than lose his night's sleep.

Here in the north of the country we found thoroughly cultivated agricultural land mixed with wooded hills, plateaus and mountain regions. An impression not expected in this part of Africa. The cultivation of this land goes back for centuries. Stone houses in the higher regions were set amidst fallowed fields. Every piece of ground around the houses was utilized for a new crop.

Under the French occupation, Algeria gained some positive influences – mainly in the agricultural sectors like its Tunisian neighbour. Algeria had since moved more towards an Islamic order than Tunisia.

The closer we came to Morocco, the more Islamic culture appeared.

On our tour we bypassed the capital Alger to avoid delays – cities always took more time to travel through. Algeria, like Libya, is a big country. You realise this when you have to travel non-stop like we did. Driver's fatigue can be dangerous when the eyelids become heavy and the neck can't stay straight. To prevent this from occurring, we stopped frequently to rest and relax.

Our time did not allow us to stay longer in Algeria. But besides Algeria, I had covered most other regions in a previous journey.

Borders in North Africa have a tendency to be located in higher regions and this was also the case with the Moroccan border.

Morocco

A bad stony road climbed up to Tlemcen. Was this a reflection of the relationship between the two countries? The border control was a smooth process – no unpacking, no piglets. Morocco had imposed a strict Arabic-Islamic order. It was no surprise that the furthest Arabic country from the centre in Mecca held the strongest Islamic tradition. It takes more time to change over a distance.

The town of Fez is an ancient settlement. Its medina (market place) was surrounded by characteristic stone walls. This was more for protection against the natural elements from the desert, such as a sand storm or a sudden deluge from a storm. A rain storm was a rare event, but we did experience this on our arrival. Everything was flooded preventing everybody from moving except in the medina. The whole spectacle lasted less than an hour and then the sun was back. The big wash-out shifted piles of mud and rubbish, partly cleaning the place but piling up somewhere else. We kept travelling after the storm and could see more flooding in the countryside. A bridge leading over a valley was engulfed by a raging torrent. We crossed this bridge without taking any precautions. We could not tell the depth of the water or the condition of the bridge. Only sheer luck helped us to get across unharmed. This raging 'wadi' could have easily washed us away beyond any help.

We were getting closer to Ceuta, the crossing point from Africa to Algeciras in southern Spain. We decided to rest for the night and cross the border in the morning.

Spain

Early the next morning we quickly made it to the border crossing and because of the crowds we were able to get through virtually uncontrolled. This allowed us to board the ship in time and before any boarding agent could demand a 'bonus' from us. Crossing the Gibraltar Straits, we welcomed the dolphins again as they raced with our ship.

European soil was reached in Algeciras. The route along the coast to Malaga broke new grounds for me. The busy roads in this fast-growing area slowed us down considerably but afforded us a magnificent view of the steep coastline, many Mediterranean bays and their blue waters. This place was an El Dorado for wealthy sun-seekers. These were probably the last frontiers in developments in Southern Europe. Malaga welcomed us with its sugar-cane fields against a background of majestic mountains. Costa Del Sol followed by Costa De La Luz, Costa Blanca and Costa Brava presented many beautiful coastal views with magnificent old Spanish cities such as Almeria, Murcia, Valencia and Barcelona. A freak storm on our arrival amidst busy traffic above the hilltops of Barcelona took us by a surprise. The wind was so strong that we had to stop the car affording us a view of the 'ocean' of city lights.

France

The French border gave us a free passage through. This was good preparation for a United Europe. Southern France followed with its wide vineyards, sand beaches along Sete, the Rhone valley to the north with its rich history of ancient Roman colonisation, especially in places like Arles, Avignon and Valence. The Southern European landscape with its rich fruit plantations in a mostly dry countryside and its strong sunshine disappeared once we passed Lyon.

Germany

The welcome on the German border became a familiar ceremony. Never before, when entering Germany, had we been asked to show our souvenirs. But this time we were told to declare all our souvenirs. Whether this border control officer had caught a 'big fish' was the question. Instead they found that we were 'little fish'. Perhaps it was because of their frustration that they demanded we pay a ridiculous amount of duty for our items. We simply could not afford this and finally told them to keep the lot. They said: "You can't do this. By law this amounts to a bribe."

We were back in the world of Germany, where everything was regulated to keep the country in a set order. Time helped to cool down the heat of this moment, allowing common sense to prevail. We finally got away with a much smaller claim, which they called a 'fine'. We could not understand their actions, but decided it was best to forget this incident so as not to spoil the success of our entire journey.

The journey around the Mediterranean Sea was, without doubt, a great success. We met people of other societies and learned more about their different conditions in life, how they respond to their environment and want to be regarded.

The world is still a rich and diverse place. We have an obligation to maintain it. There are no second chances in nature!

Back at home I had to find out if I could continue my studies. Sunday, April 23, 1967 was the date of our return. The disturbances in Heidelberg hadn't gone away. I began studies at the university as well as work to keep me going.

Impressions from the last journey soon became a distant memory with the daily demands of student life. I was still unsure about my university career and was keen to lead a more independent life. Connecting to other people in our lives can be a really good relief valve.

Stockholm, Sweden

One attempt in this direction came in early June from Stockholm in Sweden where Arja worked during a break in her studies. Her letter was the result of a joint effort with her friend Marja. The 'spark' between opposite sexes that brings them closer appeared well expressed in this letter. She was sitting on 'pins and needles' waiting for my response. My response was immediate. I took the train to Stockholm to deliver in person what I had to say. A telegram was sent to Stockholm and Finland to announce my forthcoming visit. I sent the telegram to Finland in case Arja had returned home. My telegram to Arja's family at first received a cool reception. Her father said: "Rather a Russian than a German" which meant that a Russian would be bad enough. Her father obviously had bad memories from the war.

It was interesting to see how this 'tide' could be turned around and this was achieved when I met the family later in Finland.

I met Arja in Stockholm and her friend Marja who, decades later, said: "What a beautiful love-story." On my departure from Stockholm, Arja handed me a bunch of flowers addressed to my step-mother in a preparation for her return visit.

The mail between Germany and Stockholm was very busy until the first days of August when Arja came by train. My step-parents were informed about our friendship and commented: "The Finns are also decent people."

Engagement

On her arrival in Germany, Arja telephoned first saying that she had to change trains in Heidelberg. Which party was more on tenterhooks? In the heat of the moment, I had an argument with my step-parents who would not lend me their car to pick Arja up from the station in the nearby town of Karlsruhe. My friend had the VW van nearby so I asked him for help. Arja did not mind at all what kind of car I picked her up in – it only mattered that I was the driver. We had some initial curious nervous moments when we first met. I stood my ground with Arja when we met my step-parents and together we passed this unnecessary 'examination'.

She had faced a big challenge to come out here with her little German language and therefore she mainly listened to the conversation. My step-parents' house had enough room to accommodate her. But enough formalities had happened, so the next day we decided to head to Finland to announce our engagement. 'Good recommendations' at our departure were part of their farewell: "Don't rush. Martin has still to finish his studies and you both need time to get ready for one another." I was quick to comfort them: "We can take care of ourselves, this should not become your concern. You are welcome to share our future."

Our journey to Finland in that summer turned out quite differently from my first one in the deep winter of January 1966. Long sunny hours extended now the day. Sunset took place in Finland at 11pm and sunrise at 2am.

On our stop-over in Stockholm we paid a visit to Arja's friend, Marja, who still worked in the hotel to earn money for her studies in Finland, as Arja did. During the ship passage from Stockholm through the archipelagos to Finland the sun still stood over the horizon at 10pm. The long sunset was a colourful spectacle of its own, reflecting on the sea surface.

In Finland the moment came for me to face Arja's family – this time not as a visitor but a future son-in-law. Father Petteri picked us up from the ship. All was friendly, no sign of any interrogation. I was welcomed with open arms. August 11 was chosen for our engagement date. This gave us a few days to visit family and friends.

I also had to go through the traditional Finnish 'cleaning process' – a sauna. This was a great way to become acquainted with the country and its people. Saunas sweat out all the 'bad' leaving us only clean and 'good'. Sauna is a Finnish institution. Its culture has a very positive effect on the people: straightforward, friendly, trustworthy. It takes time to call somebody a friend in Finland. When this happens, it is going to last for a lifetime. This I could not experience better than with Arja.

Turku, Finland

The family house in Auvaisberg was located outside the city of Turku in the middle of the Finnish forest, not far from the water of the Baltic Sea. The sea tributaries had numerous arms along the coastline with thousands of little islands in between. The house had an undisrupted view to the beach which was mainly rocks and not much sand. In such places the timber sauna building is next to the water so everybody can have a swim after a sauna. Glass windows in the house gave an all-year-round view of the forest and the sea.

The day of our engagement arrived. A small dinner ceremony took place first with Arja's parents, Arja and myself. The day after the wider family and friends came to celebrate with us.

Only one day before this event, I experienced some bad luck.

We were playing table tennis in the room under the house gable and occasionally we had a turn on some rope swings attached to the gable. For some stupid reason, I hit my face on the roof construction and knocked out a front tooth. A quick trip to the dentist helped to camouflage the gap in my smile with an artificial tooth. My image had been restored for the time being, but at a price. I could now prepare for our engagement day on August 11, 1967.

Finnish birch – forest

Our dinner started late in the afternoon with Arja's parents on one side of the table and us sitting opposite. I had rehearsed my speech in the Finnish language for the occasion but had a dictionary in my hand for back-up. The champagne glasses were lifted. After the first sip it was time to talk to my future in-laws: "I love your daughter, could you please give her hand in marriage?"

Before I could put my sentence together, I lost my speech. Arja helped me to finish the sentence properly. Her parents smiled and our glasses were raised again. The parents had unanimously accepted my proposal.

A long dinner continued with delight.

The next day I went with Arja into town to buy our two golden rings. An engagement party with family and friends was arranged for the following day, Saturday. I introduced myself as well as I could with Arja's assistance. A cousin brought along a guitar and this helped me overcome the language barriers.

Arja and Martin, 1967

Two years ago, Arja and I had first conversed in English. From the moment we agreed to spend our lives together, Arja began learning German, first haltingly and then improving very fast. After our engagement party we spent another week in Finland with the family. Before our departure back to Germany, a freshwater crab dinner rounded off our stay in Finland. This time Petteri tested me with the dinner drinks. Being ignorant about certain alcohol mixtures nearly inebriated me. Hardly ever drinking any alcohol, I felt terribly sick after this meal. The moment I lay down on a bed everything started turning even though my eyes were closed. My stomach announced its rebellion. I was lucky to reach the window in time.

Sleep did not help to completely restore my wellbeing. As I found out later, there were others in the same 'boat'. The day's program got spoilt. The only 'fit' people were Arja and Petteri. In patience we had to listen what Petteri had to say: "You are the weak and we are the strong ones of the family. You took it with decency, however, and did not lose your temper."

Daily life had to return in Finland and our holiday had to come to an end. It was time to start life together. To speak on my behalf, life would be much better with the support of my fiancée. We had each other, nothing much else. The starting position in our lives was equal – together we could build on it.

When the ship left Turku harbour with us on board, the whole family in Finland farewelled us. A new chapter started in both of our lives.

EPILOGUE

Life until leaving Finland with Arja could be best described as a 'lonely' life in search of direction. These years were colorful events, but the next episode would be even more colorful!

Volume II, ' Journey of a lifetime ' follows that path relating how we built on our lives from modest beginnings to mutual success.

I could not live in Finland because its cold climate throughout most of the year would have badly affected my back. Arja wanted to see the world, too. The journey began in Finland going to Germany, where we battled in vain to gain recognition.

South Africa gave us a good home for a couple of years. The political horizon told us to move on.

With family connections in Brazil we worked and lived there for some time. The country with its people was great, the problems were staggering. Returning temporarily to Germany, we gained migration approval to Australia, thus finding what we sought in our lives.

The message we received from these experiences is that nothing is perfect in this world. The journey in our lifetime has succeeded in many ways.

This story is based on true facts but some names are fictitious.

www.ingramcontent.com/pod-product-compliance
Lightning Source LLC
Chambersburg PA
CBHW030547080526
44585CB00012B/288